Modality

Central Problems of Philosophy
Series Editor: John Shand

This series of books presents concise, clear, and rigorous analyses of the core problems that preoccupy philosophers across all approaches to the discipline. Each book encapsulates the essential arguments and debates, providing an authoritative guide to the subject while also introducing original perspectives. This series of books by an international team of authors aims to cover those fundamental topics that, taken together, constitute the full breadth of philosophy.

Published titles

Causation and Explanation
Stathis Psillos

Free Will
Graham McFee

Knowledge
Michael Welbourne

Meaning
David E. Cooper

Mind and Body
Robert Kirk

Modality
Joseph Melia

Ontology
Dale Jacquette

Paradox
Doris Olin

Perception
Barry Maund

Relativism
Paul O'Grady

Scepticism
Neil Gascoigne

Truth
Pascal Engel

Universals
J. P. Moreland

Forthcoming titles

Action
Rowland Stout

God
Jay Wood

Philosophy and Science
James Logue

Realism and Anti-Realism
Stuart Brock & Edwin Mares

Rights
Duncan Ivison

Self
Stephen Burwood

Value
Chris Cherry

Modality

Joseph Melia

McGill-Queen's University Press
Montreal & Kingston • Ithaca

© Joseph Melia 2003

ISBN 0-7735-2480-0 (bound)
ISBN 0-7735-2481-9 (paper)

Published simultaneously outside North America
by Acumen Publishing Limited

McGill-Queen's University Press acknowledges the financial support of
the Government of Canada through the Book Publishing Development
Program (BPIDP) for its activities.

National Library of Canada Cataloguing in Publication Data

Melia, Joseph
    Modality / Joseph Melia.

(Central problems of philosophy)
Includes bibliographical references and index.
ISBN 0-7735-2480-0 (bound).—ISBN 0-7735-2481-9 (pbk.)

    1. Modality (Logic) 2. Modality (Theory of knowledge)
I. Title. II. Series.

BC199.M6M44 2003   160   C2003-902776-7

Designed and typeset by Kate Williams, Abergavenny.
Printed and bound by The Cromwell Press, Trowbridge.

Contents

Acknowledgements

A large number of people have not only helped to make this book possible, they have even helped to make it actual. For useful discussions in various informal meetings here at Leeds I thank Bryan Frances, Robin Le Poidevin, Andy McGonigal, Scott Shalkowski and Peter Simons. For their comments on parts of this work at various seminar presentations and informal discussions I thank Tom Baldwin, Otavio Bueno, Fiona Campbell, Chris Daly, Anthony Everett, Gordon Finlayson, Tony Halbert, Marie McGinn, Rosanna Keefe, Hugh Mellor, Adrian Moore, Alex Oliver, David Owens, Christian Piller, Becky Sharpless and Ted Sider. Tim Miller, Michael Paulin, Mark Tregear and Richard Woodward gave generous comments and corrections and provided invaluable assistance in various ways near the end. Thanks to Steven Gerrard for kind words and patience during the completion of this book, to Kate Williams for her excellent suggestions during copy-editing, to Mairi Sutherland for her useful queries during proofreading, and to an anonymous US referee for constructive and helpful criticism on the whole draft.

Thanks are also due to the AHRB, the University of York and the University of Leeds for leave granting me the time to work on and complete this book.

Finally, I give a very special thanks to Jeremy Butterfield, who was a great source of inspiration and help at the very beginning, and also to John Divers for hours of helpful discussions, conversations and generous advice.

Material from J. Melia, "Against Modalism", *Philosophical Studies* **68** (1992), 35–56 appears by kind permission of Kluwer

Academic Publishers. Material from J. Divers and J. Melia, "The Analytic Limit of Genuine Modal Realism", *Mind* 111 (2002), 15–36 is reproduced by kind permission of Oxford University Press.

1 Introduction to modality

Modality

Suppose we possessed an extraordinarily comprehensive and accurate theory of the world. Suppose that the language of this theory contained a name for every object; every single thing, from the black holes hidden in the heart of the furthest galaxies, to the fine cobwebs swaying in the corner of an attic, is mentioned by this theory. Suppose also that this theory contained a predicate for every categorical property, simple or complex, that is actually instantiated. The theory says what things are like to the highest level of detail. It tells us whether something has a mass of 1.153 kg, whether it has a charge of 4.238322 coulombs, and whether it has a length of $\sqrt{2}$ metres. Suppose, finally, that everything the theory says is true. It truly reports the colours, tones and hues of each and every pixel currently appearing on my computer screen. It truly reports the shapes, sizes, masses and charges of each and every fundamental particle in my finger.

Everything in the theory is true. But does every truth appear within the theory? Would the theory account for every single matter of fact? If such a theory ever came to be written down, could thinkers and scientists finally rest, their work finished? Let us call the view that such a theory would be complete, that every truth would appear within the theory, the categorical hypothesis. Questioning the categorical hypothesis may seem absurd. By hypothesis, the theory lists all the things that exist and truly tells us what those things are like and what relations those things bear to each other. What more could one say? What else could there be to add? And yet, a number of philosophers believe that such a theory would *not* be a theory of everything: that there is a class of truths on which this theory is simply silent – indeed, a class of truths that this theory lacks the resources to describe.

Consider the following two sentences: "Joe is tall" and "Joe is human." Both these sentences are of a simple subject–predicate form and each ascribes a categorical property to Joe. If true, they would both appear in our theory. But, on reflection, we might note that there is an important difference in the manner or mode in which Joe possesses the two properties, a distinction ignored by our supposed theory of everything. For although Joe is tall, Joe is tall only contingently or accidentally. He could have stopped growing when he was 12. He could have lost both his legs in a terrible car accident. He could have had an unfortunately close encounter with a scythe. In brief, his being tall is an accidental property of his. By contrast, given that he is human, we might think that Joe is essentially human, that humanity is a property Joe has to have. Whereas Joe could have failed to possess the property of being tall and still be the same entity – Joe – he could not have failed to possess the property of being human and still be Joe. Such distinctions between essential and accidental properties of an object are examples of *de re* modality: in these cases, it is some particular thing that has a property essentially or accidentally.

As well as there being different modes in which an object may possess a property, there are also different modes in which a proposition may be true, a distinction that is again not acknowledged by the original theory. The sentences "All bachelors are unmarried" and "All emeralds are green" are both true. Both tell us something about what things there are and what categorical properties those things have. But there is a difference in kind between these two truths. On the one hand, it is necessary that all bachelors be unmarried. It is strictly impossible for there to be a married bachelor, for the trivial reason that it is part of the meaning of "bachelor" that anything that is a bachelor be unmarried. By contrast, "All emeralds are green" is merely contingently true. It is possible that there be an emerald that was red, purple or some other colour. This distinction between contingent and necessary truths is another example of a modal distinction. Here, where the modality attaches to the proposition, the modality is said to be *de dicto*: it is the whole truth that all bachelors are unmarried that is said to be necessary. That 2 + 2 = 4, that there are no true contradictions, that nothing can be simultaneously red and green all over are all examples of truths that are necessary: they had to be true. That there are six people in this room, that some bachelors have red hair, that London is the capital of England are all truths that are contingent: they could have been otherwise.

The *de dicto* and the *de re* distinctions are related. If Joe has the property of being human essentially then it follows that the truth "Joe is human" holds of necessity. If Joe has the property of being tall contingently then the truth "Joe is tall" holds only contingently. In general, accepting that there are some properties that are held essentially and others that are held contingently entails accepting that some truths are necessary and others contingent. The converse, however, does not hold. One can believe that there are necessary truths without believing that anything has any of its properties essentially. "All bachelors are unmarried" is a necessary truth, but this does not commit us to the existence of any object that is essentially unmarried. After all, no individual person is essentially unmarried. Although everything that is a bachelor must therefore be unmarried, nobody has to be bachelor and so nobody has to have the property of being unmarried.

The kind of modal truths that will be the focus of this book are those that go beyond the merely actual and tell us something about how things might be, or must be, or would be had things been other than they actually are. On reflection, we see that our initial theory was silent about such modal truths. It only told us how things are and what categorical properties these things actually have. Those philosophers who accept modal truths believe that the initial theory, fantastically detailed as it was, falls a long way short of the desired complete and final theory.

The modal distinctions drawn above mark distinctions about the world rather than distinctions about what we know. That there could be no true contradictions is as independent of our thoughts, beliefs and desires as is the truth that the universe is expanding. Granted, there is a use of "possibly" that is epistemic rather than metaphysical; in certain contexts, when I say that tachyons are possible I mean that the existence of these things is compatible with what I know. But the distinctions between accident and essence that were drawn above are not be understood in this way. I know very well that Joe is both bald and that he is human, yet I may also believe that he could have had hair and that he must be human. And $2 + 2 = 4$ would necessarily hold whatever the state of play of my knowledge. Nor will it do to try to define possibility and necessity in terms of the a priori. For a start, the very definition of the a priori itself seems to require the modal: a sentence is a priori if it could be known without recourse to experience. But worse, it is simply an open question whether all necessary truths are knowable a priori. Goldbach's conjecture, Riemann's hypothesis and Cantor's continuum hypothesis, all presently unproved mathematical hypotheses, are all necessary truths if true at all. But whether they can be known a priori is, at the very least, an open question. It may yet be true that all necessary truths are a priori, but since this is certainly no analytic truth the concept of necessity and the a priori must be kept distinct. To accept or reject the categorical hypothesis is to take a stance on the nature of reality, not on our relation to the world.

Modality in practice

Many philosophers find the categorical hypothesis attractive. The analytic philosopher's all time favourite formal system, first-order predicate calculus, is a fine and well understood language, suited for expressing facts about what things there are and what categorical properties these things possess. It has served us well in formalizing the truths of mathematics and logic as well as the truths of science. Unfortunately, the modal truths discussed above defy the categorical hypothesis and resist formulation in first-order predicate calculus. Now, questions of essence and accident, of possibility and necessity, may seem at first to be recherché: too divorced from our everyday thought and talk to be worth much concern. Nor, one might suspect, do modal notions play a significant enough role in our philosophical theorizing to be worthy of serious attention. Perhaps we do best to preserve the categorical hypothesis, and to preserve our tried and trusted familiar formal systems by abandoning the modal altogether.[1] After all, if modal thought and talk is recherché and philosophically unimportant, then little would be lost and much would be gained by such a move.

Unfortunately, abandoning the modal is not as easy as it might at first seem. Modality is ubiquitous in both our everyday thought and talk and in our scientific and philosophical theorizing. In abandoning the modal we abandon many things that we naturally accept and think of as being trivially true or uncontentious. A philosopher who decides to abandon all talk of the temporal thereby avoids the many problems that arise in the philosophy of time, but also thereby abandons the ability to speak truly of the many uncontentious facts about time, such as that moving clocks run slow, or that John was born before Joe. Similarly, there does seem to be an abundance of uncontentious facts about the modal. Some examples are: there are many different ways the world could have been; I am unable to speak French; Joe could win his chess game in three different ways; you cannot break the laws of physics; I could have had a lot more hair than I actually do. In all these cases, we are saying things that go beyond the strictly actual and categorical. Philosophers who dare to find fault with such natural and apparently uncontentious truths had better have good reason for doing so.

Moreover, our modal thought and talk encompass far more than essence and accident – far more than possible and necessary truths. For instance, when we say that a glass is fragile, we are not saying that the glass has a certain categorical property; we are saying something about how the glass would behave in other situations, situations that may or may not actually obtain. We are saying something about how the glass would behave were it dropped, hit or treated roughly. And we take ourselves to be saying something true or false about the glass irrespective of whether or not the glass actually is dropped, hit or treated roughly. When someone says that cheap plates have a tendency to chip, again what is said seems to go beyond the strictly actual; the pronouncement is not refuted simply by showing that the object in question, as a matter of brute fact, is not chipped, for the statement says something about how cheap plates are likely to be in certain other possible situations.

Similarly, our practical reasoning involves counterfactuals: truths such as "If I had dropped the computer I would have lost a year's work" and "If Germany had invaded Britain then Germany would have won the war." Such statements are of the form "if . . . then . . .". But, as every philosophy undergraduate knows, these obvious and natural truths cannot be formalized by the logician's truth-functional →, for $A \to B$ is true if A is false – so any contrary-to-fact counterfactual comes out automatically and trivially true if translated in this way. That can't be right! These counterfactuals aren't true simply because I didn't drop the computer or because Germany didn't invade Britain. As before, counterfactuals seem to point beyond the merely actual: they tell us something about how the world would behave were it different in certain ways. They are truths that go beyond what is actually the case and the actual categorical properties and relations of the actually existing objects.

Thought and talk about the modal is widespread and pervasive. Philosophers who abandon such talk and thought find themselves at odds with common sense. Of course, common sense is not the final arbiter of truth, but a departure from common sense is nevertheless a price to pay for one's philosophy, and the greater the departure the greater the price. Of course, if it turns out that modality is incoherent or problematic, then we will have strong reasons for revising our common-sense beliefs.[2] But it would be bad methodology to begin our philosophical theorizing about a discipline by departing so radically from our everyday thought and talk.

Modality in theorizing

As well as playing a major role in our everyday thought and talk, the modal also plays a major role in our scientific and philosophical theorizing. It is part of scientific practice to ascribe dispositional properties to various objects. Scientists have discovered that salt is soluble, that hydrogen is flammable and that uranium has a tendency to decay. Such truths are modal: they do not tell us just how a thing actually is, but they tell us something about the object's tendencies or capacities. Moreover, there are many who think that science uncovers a form of natural necessity. The laws of physics are universal truths, but not *just* universal truths. It may be a universal truth that all lumps of gold are less than a mile long but this doesn't make it a law of physics. If we wished, we could construct a lump of gold that was over a mile long, although we may never actually get around to doing it. By contrast, we cannot break the laws of physics. We can respect the intuitive idea that there is a distinction of kind between a genuine law and a mere accidental generalization easily enough by invoking modal notions, perhaps by explaining how the laws support counterfactuals while the accidental generalizations do not, or by invoking a primitive notion of natural necessity that the laws possess that the accidental generalizations do not. Whichever way we go, those who would eliminate modality have difficult work cut out for them if they wish to make sense of an apparently objective distinction between laws and accidental generalizations.[3]

As well as in science, modal notions also appear to be fundamental in the study of logic. One of the main concepts (some would say the most important concept) in logic is the notion of a valid argument. What is it for an argument to be valid? Typically, the definition is in modal terms: an argument is valid if it is not possible for the premises to be true and the conclusion false.

Although this is the explanation of the general notion of validity that one finds in undergraduate textbooks, those familiar with advanced logic might resist this definition. Perhaps those taken with set-theoretic semantics would prefer to say that an argument is valid if and only if (iff) there is no model M such that the premises are true-in-M and the conclusion is false-in-M. Such a definition of validity would not use modal notions (although it would require us to believe in the existence of models). But there are problems. First, this definition is restrictive: it is restricted to those languages for which logicians have already developed a model theory. Yet it seems we can talk about validity independently of whether or not a model-theoretic semantics has been developed for the theory. Moreover, if this is all there is to the notion of validity, why should we care whether or not an argument is valid? Why should the fact that there is no set-theoretical structure that bears a particular relation to a set of sentences be anything other than a purely mathematical matter? What is to stop us giving any set-theoretic definition of "true-in-all-models" and calling this validity? Arguably, what makes a particular definition of validity important to the logician is the extent to which it captures the intuitive notion of validity. Thus Mendelson, in his textbook on mathematical logic, points to the connection between models for the predicate calculus and possible worlds.[4] Once this connection is understood we can see why the model-theoretic definition at least partly captures our intuitive notion. But the intuitive notion is there, and our formal definitions must aim to be true to it. Thus, at least at the outset, the logician must take the modal notion seriously.[5]

Modal notions have come to play a major role in philosophical theorizing. Particularly in the second half of the twentieth century, more and more philosophers have used modal concepts to solve various philosophical problems, and to provide analyses of different philosophical concepts. Of course, in philosophy, no solution and no analysis is completely uncontentious. Nevertheless, one should at least be aware of how much one has to lose by eschewing modal notions altogether. Here are some examples of how the modal can be used to help us solve problems and provide analyses.

1. The axioms of geometry appear to postulate lines that are infinitely long. Many people complain that they can find no sense in the notion of an actual infinity, but what is the alternative? Is it that lines have some arbitrary cut-off point? That if we travel far enough we shall disappear off the edge of the universe? That is even worse! There is a natural and simple solution: replace talk of the actual infinity with talk of the potential infinity. When we say that a line is infinite we don't mean that it actually stretches out for ever. Rather, for any point you might choose to travel to along a line, it is possible to have travelled a little further.

2. In logic, one expresses the limitations of formal systems by quantifying and referring to proofs. If arithmetic is consistent, then "There is no proof of the consistency of arithmetic within arithmetic" is one notorious consequence of Gödel's theorem. But for nominalists who believe only in concrete objects, this deep result is trivial. For if the nominalist is going to believe in proofs at all, they can only be concrete objects, such as marks that have actually been written down with pen on paper. But that then limits the nominalist to believing only in proofs that have actually been and (if our nominalist is a realist about the future) will be written down. That just gets Gödel wrong, for Gödel's theorem is far more interesting than the result that, as a matter of brute fact, nobody has or will prove the consistency of arithmetic within arithmetic. A Platonist has no trouble understanding Gödel because he thinks proofs are abstract entities that exist independently of our beliefs and desires; for the Platonist, all the infinitely many proofs are "out there" in

the Platonic realm. But how is the nominalist to understand Gödel's result without trivializing it?

There is an obvious and natural solution. Gödel's theorem tells us that it is not possible to prove the consistency of arithmetic within arithmetic. It is not possible to write down a series of steps that have only the axioms of arithmetic as their premises and that obey the laws of logic, and that ends with a concrete inscription asserting the consistency of arithmetic. This is surely a much more natural and intuitive way of understanding Gödel's theorem than dabbling in the Platonist's abstract realm of proofs! Yet the solution is modal: understanding Gödel's theorem in this way uses the notion of possibility.

3. Many philosophers believe that mathematics is not just a formal game: propositions such as "2 + 2 = 4" and "There are four prime numbers between 0 and 10" are, in some sense, right, while "2 + 2 = 5" and "There are no prime numbers between 0 and 10" are, in some sense, wrong. We might be tempted to call this difference truth and falsity. Unfortunately, the truth of mathematics seems to imply the existence of mathematical objects. Few philosophers are comfortable with such Platonism and it would be nice to have another solution. Perhaps what is right about the claim that there are four prime numbers between 1 and 10 is that the claim follows from the axioms of Peano arithmetic, or that, if the axioms of Peano arithmetic are true, then there are four prime numbers between 1 and 10. The trouble is, of course, that such anti-Platonist moves typically use modal notions: the "if ... then ..." cannot be a material conditional on pain of making "If Peano arithmetic is true then there are five prime numbers between 1 and 10" true, simply because of its false antecedent. Rather, the conditional must be understood as expressing a counterfactual, or a necessitation of the material conditional. Either way the relevant notion of "follows" is analysed in modal terms.[6]

4. Determinism is an important concept, both for physicists and philosophers. In the first half of the twentieth century, philosophers tried to analyse this notion in purely formal terms, largely without success. This is no surprise for it is entirely natural to spell out the notion in modal terms. Roughly, a system is deterministic if, given the starting conditions of the

system and given the laws that govern the system's behaviour, there is one and only one way in which the system could evolve.[7]

5. Anti-realism. Philosophers spend hours debating issues that cannot easily be resolved. Is there an external world or are we only dreaming? Did anything exist before the universe was created? Do green things seem to you the way blue things seem to me? Various anti-realists try to cut through the debate by arguing that, despite appearances, there is nothing to argue about. The question of whether there is really an external world, over and above what we perceive, is not a meaningful one for the reason that it is impossible to prove it: it is not a testable hypothesis. In this way, certain anti-realists allow as meaningful or significant only those propositions that we can know or verify.

Testability, verifiability and knowability are all modal notions. Yet the modality is essential; we cannot, for example, replace the knowable with the known. After all, if the positivist rules that a proposition is meaningless simply because it is not known, then any debate over a currently unresolved issue turns out to be a meaningless one. As such, the anti-realist cannot make sense of any kind of enquiry. If the anti-realist wants his position to be at all plausible then he had better formulate his position using modality.

6. Supervenience. Many philosophers believe that there is an intimate connection between the mental and the physical. In some sense, the mental is nothing more than the physical. Philosophers used to try to spell out the relation in terms of reduction: all our mental talk could be paraphrased into physical talk. Unfortunately, we can now see that such an ambitious project is not achievable. Accordingly, the nature of the intimate connection has to be spelled out some other way. Philosophers have used the notion of supervenience as their account of the relationship between the mental and the physical. But supervenience is a modal notion: to say that the mental supervenes upon the physical is to say that it is not possible for two things to share all the same physical properties without sharing the same mental properties.

Modal scepticism and modal anti-realism

For all that has been said above, there are philosophers who have expressed scepticism about the modal. What I have said so far will not reassure a modal sceptic. But do we need to refute modal scepticism before we begin the philosophical study of modality? After all, there are philosophers who have also expressed scepticism about the existence of the external world. As too many philosophers have shown, it is relatively easy to express scepticism about just about any position one likes and to formulate one's scepticism in such a way that the scepticism cannot be refuted. But just because one can adopt a sceptical attitude, just because the sceptic cannot be convinced of the reality of the external world, does not mean that we should give up our belief in the existence of the external world, or that it is irrational to begin studying physics until such scepticism has been refuted. To show the irrationality of empirical enquiry we need a sceptical argument: an argument that begins with premises that we believe, that uses modes of inference that we accept and whose conclusion is that we do not have the modal knowledge that we usually take ourselves to have. And, as yet, this is not something that the modal sceptics have provided.

What is true is that, at least in some cases, our modal knowledge falls on the wrong side of the a priori/a posteriori distinction. Our knowledge that Joe is bald is a posteriori: we find this out by observing Joe. But once we have this piece of knowledge, our knowledge that Joe is merely contingently bald seems to be a priori. There's no further observation we make to find out that Joe has his baldness contingently. However, the existence of substantive or synthetic a priori knowledge is contentious. Empiricists think there is no such thing: all genuine, synthetic knowledge must come through the senses. The fact that the existence of such modal knowledge is not compatible with empiricism is, at the very least, enough to put supporters of the modal in an uncomfortable position. Of course, all but the most radical believe in some a priori knowledge: all bachelors are unmarried, all unicorns have horns. But the empiricist will regard such truths as analytic – true simply because of the meanings of the terms, or true simply in virtue of the way we use words. If the necessary truths really owe their necessity to the fact that the truths are analytic, then the necessary/contingent distinction appears to be nothing more than a semantic issue, and not a topic for serious metaphysical debate.

Such epistemological problems should not be dismissed lightly. But they are far from conclusive. Empiricism is itself contentious, and there is little agreement about how it should be understood. On the one hand, if we take empiricism strictly and say that we should only count as knowledge those propositions that we can immediately observe to be true, then we run the risk of discounting many beliefs that we do want to count as knowledge. We cannot directly see the future, we cannot directly observe quarks and electrons, we cannot directly see that something is a law of nature, yet to conclude that we cannot have knowledge of the future, of quarks and electrons, and of laws of nature is an overreaction. It is more plausible to think that the philosopher who espouses such a strict empiricism has erred than that we do not know that the sun will rise tomorrow. On the other hand, if we take empiricism loosely, and admit truths that can be indirectly confirmed or justified, then we run the risk of bringing the modal back in, for we do have plenty of good evidence that glasses are fragile, that uranium tends to decay and that if I drop the computer it will fall down the stairs rather than levitate in the air. These truths may not be directly observable, but nor do we come to know them simply by closing our eyes and thinking. Empirical evidence exists that supports all these propositions. The empiricist, then, has some way to go before he is in a position to justify his scepticism about the modal, let alone in a position to justify his empiricism.

Paraphrase

Another deflationary response to the modal is to claim that modal thought and talk can be paraphrased away. After all, we ought not to treat our ordinary thought and talk with too much respect. For instance, there is plenty of ordinary thought and talk that seem to concern the average man. We say that the average man has 2.4 children, that the average man is living longer than he used to and that the average man is taller than he used to be, but it would be absurd to think that, if we are to take such thought and talk seriously, there must exist some entity in the world that is the average man. Of course, it turns out that our talk of the average man can be easily paraphrased away. "The average man has 2.4 children" can be seen as just a convenient way of saying "The number of children divided by the number of men is 2.4", which sentence doesn't involve any such strange thing as the average man. Our thought and talk about average men can be seen as a convenient way of thinking or speaking, as nothing more than a *façon de parler*.

Unfortunately, it is no easy matter to paraphrase away our modal talk, or reduce modal truths to truths about what things there are and what properties and relations these things instantiate. Let us here just consider dispositions as an example. Quine, a friend of natural science but an enemy of the modal, once suggested that "y is soluble" be paraphrased as "$\forall x(x$ has an internal structure like y, y has been placed in water, y has dissolved)". The paraphrase uses no modal notions: it talks only of what there is, what has happened and what properties actual things possess. But as a paraphrase it faces overwhelming objections. First, two things may share a dispositional property and yet have quite different internal structures. Nuclear bombs and Semtex both have a tendency to explode, but the internal structures of these things are very different. Secondly, as many have argued, such an account does not allow for the genuine possibility of unmanifested dispositions. Salt would still be soluble whether or not it, or any other substance, had ever been placed in water. Yet, for Quine's paraphrase to work, there must be at least one substance that actually has been placed in water and actually has dissolved. Quine later went on to suggest that dispositional terms did not, after all, belong to scientific discourse but were introduced only while science was incomplete. Only while scientists do not know the chemical or physical features of salt that are responsible for its solubility must they talk of the solubility of salt. Even so, the actual practice of working physicists and the actual content of current physics appear to use modal terms. In so far as one adopts a naturalistic attitude towards science and eschews first philosophy, as Quine tells us we should, it is hard to see what justifies Quine's attitude towards dispositional terms. Moreover, there seems to be no reason to think that dispositions will be eliminated should science ever be completed. With the advent of irreducibly probabilistic physics, such as quantum theory, it is possible that, at the fundamental level, there is nothing more to say about the basic kinds of entities than that they have certain irreducible tendencies and dispositions to behave in certain ways under certain conditions.

Anti-realism

Another form of scepticism comes from those who think that the modal is unknowable because, strictly speaking, there is nothing about the modal to know. Although I have shown the ubiquity of our modal thought and talk, perhaps it is a mistake to construe this as being about a mind-independent objective reality. Perhaps modal statements are not true independently of our beliefs and desires. Perhaps they are not even true at all. Perhaps the distinction between the contingent and necessary merely reflects a distinction in our attitudes towards these statements. The view that Joe is essentially human is not to be thought of as the objective fact that Joe possesses humanity in a some peculiarly special way, an essential way. Rather, we simply wouldn't call anything "Joe" if it wasn't human. Perhaps the fact that we call the truths of mathematics necessary reflects not an objective feature of the world, but rather a convention to hold these statements true come what may. Perhaps we should be anti-realists about the modal.

As with scepticism, so with anti-realism. It is possible to be an anti-realist about almost any body of discourse one chooses. In some cases, anti-realism is plausible. It is hard to believe that there are objective truths about what is funny, truths that hold independently of our beliefs and our desires. Different people have different senses of humour, and it seems strange to believe that one person is right and another wrong about what is funny. By contrast, it is plausible that there are objective truths about tables and chairs, about sub-atomic particles, and the far-flung reaches of the universe. When we say that a particular table has four legs, we do not naturally take ourselves to be reporting something subjective, something that depends on perceivers or believers, or communities thereof. And, modal realists argue, our thought and talk about the modal has a similar character. When we say that the computer would fall if it were dropped, the truth of this statement does not seem to depend upon anything about us. The glass would still be fragile whether or not anybody was around to believe it. Uranium retains its tendency to decay independently of what we think or do. And it is not easy to believe that, if we had willed otherwise or adopted a different convention, $2 + 2$ would have been anything other than 4. Moreover, the very definition of anti-realism itself arguably requires modal concepts; if this requires the anti-realist to be anti-realist about anti-realism then his position is in danger of becoming incoherent.

The opponents of modality will, quite rightly, respond that just noting that anti-realism is unjustified is not enough to justify realism. This is a fair comment. However, there is something in our everyday thought and talk that favours modal realism. We are accustomed to making modal claims; we reason and argue about the truth of counterfactuals; we give evidence to support our view about somebody's capacities; we think we have good reason to believe that uranium has a tendency to decay; we can enter into reasoned debate about whether or not the laws of logic are necessary or contingent. Unlike the question of whether or not something is funny, when we enter such debates we appear to be arguing something substantive and real. Someone who thinks that the computer would not fall when dropped, but would levitate in the air, seems not merely to have a different modal taste from myself but to be making a genuine mistake. Moreover, while our talk of what is funny has no positive place in a scientific or metaphysical theory, we have already seen that the modal may well earn its place in our scientific or metaphysical theories. Those who wish to be anti-realists about the modal may end up being anti-realist about a lot more than they would desire.

None of these considerations refutes the anti-realist position, but they do at least suggest that, without some argument or reason for anti-realism in modality, our presumption is positive. Of course, it may be that, as we study the modal, features are revealed that turn out to justify such an anti-realism. But such a decision can only be reached after a serious investigation of the modal.

Strengths of modality

We have already seen that, in everyday practice, the word "possibly" can be used in two ways. On the one hand, there is the epistemic reading of "possibly *P*", which we use to say which propositions we cannot rule out, given what we know. On the other hand, there is a metaphysical use of the term that we take to be answerable to an external reality. But there is reason to think that the word is used to cover a whole plethora of concepts. For instance, when assessing the plausibility of *Star Trek*, we might point out that a starship flying at warp speed is crazy: it is not possible for anything to travel faster than the speed of light. And anyone who responded that the laws of physics are themselves contingent would seem to be missing the point. Sure, it is *logically* possible that things travel faster than light, but it is not *physically* possible. Finding me in France, someone might ask me for directions. I might excuse myself and say that it is not possible for me to give him directions in French. If my questioner angrily responds that I have a normal brain, that I could have paid more attention in French at school, that I could have attended a refresher course before my visit to France, and thus that of course it is possible for me to give my answers in French, he would again seem to be missing my point. "Yes", I might say, "of course it's possible for me to speak French, but I'm afraid that it's not possible *for me*." Such elasticity in our talk about what is possible might worry us that our ordinary thought and talk about the modal is simply confused, vague or incoherent. A modal sceptic or anti-realist might seize on such a fact to suggest that, as such, our modal practices do not latch on to reality.

But this would be an overreaction. It is not that our modal thought and talk are confused but that, in different contexts, different facts are being kept fixed and, relative to those facts, different propositions are possible. When we say that the Starship Enterprise cannot go faster than light we are fixing the physical laws and saying that the ship's travelling at warp speed is not compatible with these laws. Similarly, when I explain that I cannot speak French I am keeping certain facts about my past fixed. These facts are not necessary – I could have had a different past where I learned French – but given that my interrogator is expecting an explanation *now* I take such possibilities to be irrelevant to the context of the question. When I reply that I cannot speak French I am keeping these facts fixed and explaining that it is not compatible with such facts that I now answer in French.

We might regiment these related senses of possibility by introducing different terms into our philosophical system. We might have one notion for metaphysical possibility, another for physical possibility, another for psychological possibility and so on. For all the various notions of possibility we find ourselves needing, we might introduce some primitive notion. However, such a proposal would not be ideologically parsimonious. Indeed, the preceding paragraph suggests how these various strengths of modality could be defined in terms of each other. Instead, we take certain collection of truths as given – call these the φ truths – and then define the notion of φ-possibility as "compatible with the φ truths". So, for example, the notion of physically possible becomes "compatible with the laws of nature", biologically possible becomes "compatible with the laws of biology", and so on. In this way, the various strengths of modality can be captured and represented in a simple and natural way using only the notion of compatibility.

One might wonder whether *all* our notions of possibility and necessity are relative to some collection of truths we have decided to keep fixed. Perhaps, by following through the project just outlined, there is no need to believe in any kind of absolute necessity or contingency at all. However, this is far too quick, for the definitions of various kinds of possibility all used the notion of compatibility. And, at least at first sight, *compatibility* is itself a modal notion: P is compatible with Q if it is possible for P and Q to be true together. If the above definitions of the various kinds of possibility are to be unambiguous and understood in a simple and unified manner, then there had better be a clear and unequivocal notion of compatibility at work here.

Reflection suggests that we do have a notion of absolute necessity. True, with the physical laws fixed, it is not physically possible for anything to travel faster than the speed of light. But we do not think that the physical laws themselves are absolutely necessary. True, with the biological facts fixed, it is not biologically possible for me to have had different genes. But the biological laws themselves are contingent. True, with the laws of arithmetic fixed, it is not possible for $2 + 2$ to be anything but 4. But the laws of arithmetic themselves are not contingent. $2 + 2$ has to be 4: it absolutely couldn't be any other number. The laws of arithmetic have to have the form that they do: they couldn't be any other way. True, with the laws of logic fixed, it follows that there are no true contradictions. But the laws of logic themselves are *not* contingent: the laws themselves (absolutely) could not be any other way.

There are indeed many forms of necessity. But many can be defined in terms of what is (absolutely) compatible with a certain set of facts, which we have arbitrarily decided to keep fixed.

Throughout, a particular kind of necessity – absolute necessity – is needed to define these various relative modalities. Moreover, the mere notion of relative modality is not enough to capture a distinction that we want to capture: a distinction in kind between the laws of logic and the laws of biology; a distinction in kind between the laws of mathematics and the laws of physics – a distinction between what is absolutely necessary and what is absolutely contingent.

Possible worlds

Earlier I pointed out that modal truths seem to violate the hypothesis that the complete theory of everything would involve only truths of the form "*a* is *F*", "*a* bears *R* to *b*" and so on. That Joe has the property of being human essentially seems to be a truth that goes beyond which things there are and what properties these things have. A description that contained only sentences such as *Fa*, *Rab* and $\forall x F x$ would be incomplete: it would not tell us whether *a* is necessarily *F*, or whether it is necessary that there is something that is *F*. In some sense, modal truths seem to go beyond such straightforward categorical truths.

However, many workers in modality think that realism about such modal truths is not best understood as the view that what were missing from such a categorical description were further truths about the necessary and the contingent; rather, what were missing were further truths about what things existed. The categorical descriptions considered above told us only what existed, and the way these things were, in the actual world. For the description to be really complete, it would have to tell us what existed and the way these things were in *other possible worlds*. Such possible worlds are to be thought of as complete ways that reality might have been. For every meaningful, factual proposition one might care to consider, no matter how small the detail, no matter how remote the subject matter, there is a possible world that makes that proposition true or false. Only when we have a categorical description that includes not only what happens here, at the actual world, but also tells us what happens at other possible worlds, would our description tell us which truths are necessary and which are contingent. Necessarily, 2 + 2 = 4 because not only does 2 + 2 = 4 at the actual world, but 2 + 2 = 4 at every possible world. I am necessarily human because not only am I human at the actual world, but I am human at every possible world at which I exist. It is possible that there are unicorns because there is a possible world at which unicorns exist.

At first glance, this idea strikes us as monstrous. The belief that "Joe is tall" is contingently true seems relatively uncontentious, a fact scarcely worth mentioning at all and, at least at first sight, unproblematic. By contrast, the belief that there are possible worlds other than the actual one is outrageous. Yet the proposal here is to understand truths of the first sort as really being truths of the second sort.

Despite its apparent implausibility, the view that a commitment to possible worlds gives us the best way of understanding modality has become something of an orthodoxy. And, as we shall see, bizarre though this view may be, the hypothesis that there is a plurality of worlds has indeed shed light upon the concept of modality, and provides us with a way of unifying very many different modal notions. Such unification is best illustrated by an example.

Possible worlds can be used to analyse counterfactuals: sentences of the form "If P had been the case then Q would have been the case." In a modal logic, the concept of necessity and the concept of a counterfactual are not definable in terms of each other. A modal language that could represent both concepts would need two new primitives: the one-place connective, $\Box$, to represent necessity, and the two-place connective, $\Box\!\!\rightarrow$, to represent the counterfactual. However, with the machinery of possible worlds, both can be represented using the familiar predicate calculus. Necessity is understood as what is the case at all possible worlds: P is necessarily true iff it is true at all possible worlds. Counterfactuals are understood by considering what is the case at close possible worlds: if P were true then Q would be true iff, at the closest possible world in which P is true, Q is true.

Simplicity in a theory is a virtue. The simpler the ontology, the fewer the primitives, the better the theory. It is true that accepting an ontology of possible worlds seems ontologically unparsimonious (although, as we shall see, many a possible worlds theorist argues that the ontology is not quite as bad as it might at first appear). But this is counterbalanced, at least in part, by the ideological economy that possible worlds provide, an instance of which is given by the way in which possible worlds can treat both the notions of necessity and of counterfactuals without having to postulate any further primitive notions.[8]

Even so, the reader might protest, gains of theoretical economy may seem like scant consolation compared with the outrageous ontology of possible worlds. To believe in an infinity of possible worlds containing unicorns, centaurs, spirits and minds is outrageous. The whole metaphor of possible worlds is nothing more than that: a mere metaphor, an heuristic that should not be elevated to a literal truth. It is certainly true that the hypothesis that there exists a plurality of worlds is not plausible. However, it should be noted that, so far, nothing has been said as to the nature of these possible worlds. True, if the possibility of P is to be analysed in terms of the existence of some world at which P is true, then we know that there are an extremely large number of these things. However, this basic idea in no way commits us to the thought that other possible worlds are like the actual ones, that they contain other flesh and blood beings going about their various activities. In its purest form, the idea that "It is possible that P" is to be treated as "There is a possible world at which P", commits us to a possible world at which P is true, but leaves it completely open what possible worlds are, and in virtue of what P is true at a world. Perhaps possible worlds are really nothing more than books, and P is true at a world in much the same way as "Holmes is a detective" is true in *The Scarlet Band*. Perhaps possible worlds are really nothing more than pictures, and P is true at a world in much the same way as "The cavalier is laughing" is true according to the well-known painting. Or perhaps possible worlds are really nothing more than sets of propositions, and P is true at a world simply when the proposition P is a member of that world. Whatever the correct account turns out to be, we can see that accepting possible worlds analyses allows us a degree of flexibility in the theory of possible worlds we ultimately choose. A good deal of this book will be spent exploring some of these options.

Modal language and
2 | modal logic

In this chapter we meet the modal languages and modal logics that philosophers and logicians use to formalize modal thought and talk. In order to understand the significance of the model theory for modal languages, we shall also examine model theory for non-modal first-order language. Finally, we'll see that there are limitations to the expressive resources of these modal systems: certain natural modal theses cannot be expressed in straightforward modal languages – although they *can* be expressed in a first-order language that quantifies over worlds and possibilia. This will be the first sign of support for possible worlds theory.

Quantified modal language

Some philosophers think that *any* fact can be captured in a language containing only names and predicates. Others argue that there are some true thoughts whose correct expression involves quantification over things – and *only* things: the first-order predicate calculus is the correct logical framework. Still others believe that, since first-order formulations of mathematical theories such as arithmetic and set theory have clearly non-standard models, second-order logic is required.[1] And yet others maintain that none of these languages is capable of expressing modal facts.[2]

First- and second-order languages have been extensively studied by logicians. These languages can be presented in formal systems whose grammatical and syntactical rules are precisely defined. Deductive systems for these logics have also been studied and there exist precisely defined semantic systems for these logics.[3] Students and researchers alike are well trained at translating English sentences into first-order languages, and sentences of first-order languages into English. This leads us to feel that we have a good grasp of these different languages: that we have a good grasp of what is expressible in these various languages and what the expressive limits of these languages are. We also know what concepts the different languages take as primitive, and this enables philosophers to focus on what may be obscure or contentious in a new language. Even opponents of second-order languages welcome the formalization and regimentation of second-order logic and the presentation of a precise syntax and semantics, for whether attacking or defending a particular position, the position under consideration should be well defined so that its strengths and weaknesses can be located. If the formulation of modal truth does indeed force us to go beyond the limits of the philosopher's familiar non-modal languages then, at the very least, we need the unfamiliar terrain to be mapped out so we can assess it properly. We need a precise modal language so we know exactly what the language is capable of doing and what its limitations are. Let us see what a precise modal language looks like.

QML: a precise modal language

Let us begin by recalling the first-order predicate calculus with identity. The vocabulary of the first-order predicate language contains as its basic items the following:

(a) the connectives $\neg$, $\&$, $\rightarrow$ and $\vee$
(b) the quantifiers $\forall$ and $\exists$
(c) the variables $x_1, x_2, \ldots, x_n, \ldots$
(d) the predicate letters $F, G, H, \ldots$
(e) the two-place predicate $=$
(f) the names $a, b, c, \ldots$
(g) the brackets (and).

These items are to be thought of as the "letters" of the language.

The predicate calculus also contains rules for which strings of letters are well formed. We are familiar with sensible strings of symbols, such as $Fa \,\&\, Gb$ and $\forall x \exists y Rxy$, but any old string of symbols does not count as a well-formed formula of the language. For example, $aF{\rightarrow}x\exists$ is ungrammatical: this particular string of symbols is not well formed. Intuitively, the difference between well-formed and badly formed formulas is that the former will "make sense" while the latter will "be gibberish". But our intuitive concept of "makes sense" is too vague to be used in a foundation for logic – particularly in modal logic, where people's intuitions may not be clear cut. We would like a definition of *well-formed formula* in purely formal terms. Such a formal presentation can be done inductively as follows.

First, call the variables and names the *terms* of our language.

Secondly, say that any n-place predicate letter of first-order calculus concatenated with n terms yields the *atomic formulas*. That is, if F is an n-place predicate letter and $t_1, \ldots, t_n$ are terms, then $F(t_1, \ldots, t_n)$ is an atomic formula.

The *well-formed formulas (wffs) of the first-order predicate calculus* are then inductively defined as follows:
1. Every atomic formula is a wff.
2. If φ and ψ are wffs and y is a variable, then $\neg\varphi$, $\varphi \mathbin{\&} \psi$, $\varphi \rightarrow \psi$, $\varphi \vee \psi$, $\exists y\varphi$ and $\forall y\varphi$ are all wffs.
3. An expression is a wff only if it can be shown to be a wff on the basis of 1 and 2.

In order to reach a quantified *modal* language, we first add two new operators, $\Box$ and $\Diamond$ (pronounced "necessarily" and "possibly") to the vocabulary of the first-order predicate calculus.[4] Secondly, we add a new one-place predicate, E, for existence. When talking about modality, we often wish to talk about things that might or might not have *existed*; although such talk can be captured in the resources we already have, it can be represented more perspicuously with this new predicate E. Ea can be thought of as saying "a exists". Accordingly, the vocabulary of quantified modal logic, as well as containing clauses (a)–(g) above, also contains:

(h) the operators $\Box$ and $\Diamond$
(i) the one-place predicate letter E.

As before, it is not enough simply to know what the letters of our quantified modal language are. To complete the presentation, we have to know which strings of letters are wffs and which strings are not. Formally, the two operators □ and ◊ are treated as being grammatically like the negation symbol. Just as in the predicate calculus, where we can put a negation symbol in front of the wffs *Fa*, *Rxy*, and *Rxy* → *Gb* to form new wffs ¬*Fa*, ¬*Rxy* and ¬(*Rxy* → *Gb*), so in quantified modal language we can put the necessarily and possibly symbols in front of these wffs to form the new wffs ◊*Fa*, ◊*Rxy*, ◊(*Rxy* → *Gb*), □*Fa*, □*Rxy* and □(*Rxy* → *Gb*). More formally we say:

> The *terms* of quantified modal language are the variables and the names.[5]
>
> Any predicate letter of quantified modal language applied to the terms results in an *atomic formula*.[6]
>
> *The wffs of quantified modal language* are then given as follows:
> 1. Every atomic formula is a wff.
> 2. If φ and ψ are wffs and *y* is a variable, then ¬φ, φ & ψ, φ → ψ, φ ∨ ψ, ∃*y*φ, ∀*y*φ, □φ and ◊φ are all wffs.
> 3. An expression is a wff only if it can be shown to be a wff on the basis of 1 and 2.

Examples of wffs of quantified modal language are: ◊*Fx*, □(F_a → F_c) and ∀*x*□∃*y*(*x* = *y*). Examples of formulas that are not well formed are: *F*□*x*, ∀◊(*Fy* → *Fz*) and *Fx* & *Fy*◊.

We call this language quantified modal logic, or QML. Let's see the language in action by translating a couple of English modal sentences into QML. "It is necessary that all bachelors are unmarried" can be expressed by the formula □(∀*x*(*Bx* → ¬*Mx*)), where *Bx* is "*x* is a bachelor" and *Mx* is "*x* is married". In general, provided that the non-modal sentence φ can be expressed in the first-order predicate calculus, "it is necessary that φ" is expressed by □φ.

Similarly, "It is possible that Joe could have been seven feet tall" is expressed by the formula ◊*Fa* where *Fx* is "*x* is seven feet tall" and *a* refers to Joe.

"It is *contingent* that φ" can be expressed in QML (provided, of course, that φ itself can be expressed in QML), for a proposition is contingent iff (i) it could have been true and (ii) it could have been false. Thus we can say that it is contingent that Joe is six feet tall by writing ◊*Ga* & ◊¬*Ga*, where *Gx* is "*x* is six feet tall" and *a* again refers to Joe. In general, the contingency of a proposition φ will be expressed by ◇φ & ◇¬φ.

More complex thoughts, such as "John could have had a brother who might have been an astronaut" can be written as ◇∃x(Rxa & ◇Fx), where *a* is our name for John, *Rxy* is "*x* is the brother of *y*" and *Fx* is "*x* is an astronaut".

QML: some concerns

One of the oldest modal topics to concern philosophers was the distinction between properties that are held *essentially* and those that are held *contingently*. But expressing this distinction in QML is not straightforward. A first attempt to say that there exists something that has the property of *F*-ness *essentially* might take the form ∃x□Fx – in English, "There exists an *x* such that, necessarily, *x* is *F*." Similarly, we might try to say that something has the property of being *F* contingently using the formula ∃x(◇Fx & ◇¬Fx) – in English, "There exists an *x* such that it is possible for that *x* to be *F* and it is possible for that *x* to be not *F*." But it is not easy to see whether these formalizations are correct. There are two related worries we might have about these attempts to formalize the distinction between essential and contingent properties.

1. Does the grammatical structure of QML have sufficient flexibility to express the relevant distinction correctly? In English, we say "There is something that is necessarily human." The word "necessarily" occurs between the words "is" and "human". In so occurring, it appears to be saying something about the *way* in which some *x* is human, and so makes it clear that it is saying something about the relation between the object *x* and its humanity. In QML, we might intuitively want to reflect this fact by placing the □ *between* the *x* and the *F* to write something like ∃x(x□F). But this is not a well-formed string of symbols in QML. So we cannot place the □ where, intuitively, we wish to. Because of the limitations of the grammatical rules of QML, we are forced to say "There is an *x* such that, necessarily, *x* is *F*", and it is not immediately clear that saying *this* has the same effect as saying that there is an *x* that is essentially *F*.

2. The proposition that there is something that has a property essentially does *not* imply that anything exists necessarily. Joe may be essentially human: he could not have existed without being human. But it doesn't follow from this that Joe *must* exist. Despite having his humanity essentially, Joe himself is still a contingent being and, had things been different, he might not have existed at all. Accordingly, when we say that something has an essential property, we don't want to imply that it exists necessarily. However, it is not clear that the formula $\exists x \Box Fx$ avoids this trap. For instance, one might argue as follows:

> $\exists x \Box Fx$ says that there is some x such that necessarily x is human. If true, then there is something that satisfies the open formula $\Box Fx$; let us call this thing a. Then it follows that, necessarily, a is human. But a's being human entails that a exists, for how could something be human and yet not exist? So, necessarily, if a is human then a exists. Now, if P is necessarily true and if "if P then Q" is necessarily true, it follows that Q is necessarily true. Letting $P = a$ is human and $Q = a$ exists, it follows that a exists necessarily.

It is not at all clear where, if anywhere, this argument goes wrong.[7] But if the argument is correct then our formula, $\exists x \Box Fx$, is too strong: it not only implies that there is something that is necessarily F, but it implies that that something exists necessarily.[8]

Even when we consider examples of sentences that do not include quantifiers, the solutions to these difficulties is still unclear. Again, at a purely intuitive level, we might like to have formalized "Joe is necessarily human" by the ill-formed formula $a\Box F$, placing the $\Box$ between the name and the predicate. But the closest wff that our modal language permits us to form here is $\Box Fa$. As before, one might well worry that this sentence says too much, committing us to the necessity of a's existence.

Moreover, such formulations don't seem to enable us to distinguish between *de re* and *de dicto* truths. Recall that *de re* propositions, such as "Joe is necessarily human", say something about the way in which a particular object instantiates a property, while *de dicto* propositions, like "Necessarily all bachelors are unmarried", ascribe a necessity to the proposition as a whole rather than any particular individual or object. The grammar of QML doesn't seem to be sensitive to such distinctions. Is □*Fa* to be read as a *de dicto* or a *de re* sentence? On the face of it, it looks *de dicto*: it can be read as saying that the proposition *a* is *F* is necessary. But we wanted to give it a *de re* reading: the object *a* is necessarily *F*. Perhaps, when the term in a particular sentence is a name, the distinction between the *de re* and *de dicto* readings doesn't amount to very much. But if the term is a *description* then we do seem to face difficulties. Consider the sentence "The tallest man is necessarily human." Suppose we expand our quantified modal language so that it contains a term, *t*, which we take to mean "the tallest man". Then, in our expanded quantified modal language the sentence would be written □*Ft*, where *Fx* is "*x* is human". Translating □*Ft* back into English gives us "Necessarily, the tallest man is human." But now something is wrong. This truth is trivial. The tallest man is human simply by definition, so of course it is necessary that the tallest man is human. This *de dicto* proposition was not what we were originally trying to assert. Rather, we were trying to make the more contentious *de re* claim that the tallest man, in and of himself, no matter how you referred to him, was *essentially* human. Our extended quantified modal language just doesn't seem to be capable of making the relevant distinction.[9]

Such difficulties of interpretation are cause for concern. The modal thoughts that we are trying to express in our formalized language do not seem to be particularly complicated. Yet already we find ourselves facing serious difficulties assessing just what modal thought a particular sentence of our quantified modal language expresses. Moreover, with neither a semantics nor a deductive system for our modal language, the only way we have of checking our translations is an appeal to our intuitions, intuitions that, as the difficulties above show, are none too clear.

Problems with QML do not end there. Recall that, according to our rules, □ and ◊ behave just like the negation symbol. This means that, if φ is a wff then so are □φ and ◊φ. But if □φ is a wff then, according to the rule, □□φ and ◊□φ are wffs too. Indeed, it turns out that the rules allow all manner of strange beasts to count as wffs. ◊◊φ,

◇◇◇◇◇◇◇◇◇◇φ and ◇◇□◇◇□¬□◇◇◇◇φ → ◇□◇◇□□◇◇◇□φ, are just a few of the wffs of QML. Yet these sentences are mind-boggling. True, even in the non-modal propositional case, we can produce sentences that are difficult to grasp: "¬ ¬ ¬ ¬ ¬ ¬ ¬ ¬ ¬ ¬ ¬ ¬grass is green" is not the easiest sentence to understand. Nevertheless, given a little time and patience, we know how to work out what it says, and we can work out under what conditions it is true. But even a single iteration of the modal operators produces a sentence that is baffling. While we may have fairly firm beliefs as to whether or not P is necessary, many of us find ourselves at a complete loss when wondering whether or not P is *necessarily* necessary. Intuitively, it may not even be immediately clear to us whether such a proposition makes sense.

There is a deeper reason for this. When we first met the topic of modality, the topic was introduced by pointing towards a difference in the *way* in which different objects could instantiate different properties. Although Joe instantiates both the properties of being bald and being human, there is an intuitive distinction in the *way* in which Joe instantiates these two properties. While Joe instantiates the property of being bald *contingently*, he instantiates the property of being human *necessarily*. Similarly, there are two ways in which a proposition can be true: the propositions "Socrates is snubnosed" and "2 + 2 = 4" are both true, but the first is true *contingently* while the second is true *necessarily*. However, if this is our basic understanding of modality, then it is no surprise that we find iterated modalities confusing. If our understanding of modality is essentially adverbial, then iterating an adverb typically results in nonsense. For instance, we can distinguish different ways in which people can run. Some people run slowly while other people run quickly. But it is senseless to say that somebody runs quickly quickly. We have no trouble understanding different ways of running, but what could be meant by different ways of different ways of running is obscure.

We might try to respond to this worry by adjusting the inductive rules for when it is that a formula is well formed. If the wffs of QML turn out to be gibberish then the rules of well-formedness must be changed. But drawing a logical line between the grammatical and the ill formed turns out to be difficult. For instance, one natural solution would be to say that ◇φ and □φ are wffs iff φ is a wff *containing no modal operators*. Doing this would certainly eliminate the problematic formulas involving iterated modal operators considered above but, unfortunately, it would eliminate too much. For there are contexts in which we want to talk about the modal properties of merely possible objects and the formulation of such theses involves nesting modal operators within the scope of others. For instance, Joe could have had a brother. Any such brother would instantiate certain properties: he would be a certain height, he would be a certain weight, and he would have a particular birthday. He would also have had certain modal properties: he would have had his height contingently, and his humanity essentially. Accordingly, Joe could have had a brother who was necessarily human. In order to formulate this in our formal language, modal operators have to appear within the scope of another modal operator: $\Diamond[\exists x(Bjx \ \& \ \Box Hx)]$. But if we accept the rule that $\Diamond\varphi$ is well formed iff φ contains no modal operators, then this formula is *not* well formed in our language. This is intolerable. Our formal modal language has to be capable of expressing all the modal theses we wish to express if it is going to be a suitable vehicle for formulating the truth about the modal.

It is not at all clear how and where the line between sense and nonsense is to be drawn. If we allow the modal operators the same syntactic freedom as the negation symbol, then we generate sentences that are almost impossible to understand or assess and that, we fear, may be nothing more than nonsense. Yet we must be careful not to restrict these operators too far, else we will find our language unable to express natural modal theses. We never had this problem in non-modal quantified logic, where it was quite clear what the syntactic behaviour of the logical constants should be. And the fact that we have a clear grip of how these constants should behave indicates how well understood they are. It is one thing to show some understanding of a certain range of modal sentences, but if we do not even know how to fix the syntactic behaviour of the modal operators then can we really be confident that we have such a great understanding of these operators? The logician's choice has been to allow the modal operators the freedom of the negation symbol. Accordingly, the strange string $\Diamond\Diamond\Box\Diamond\Diamond\Box\neg\Box\Diamond\Diamond\Diamond\Diamond\varphi \rightarrow \Diamond\Box\Diamond\Diamond\Box\Box\Diamond\Diamond\Diamond\Box\varphi$ is well formed. But this still leaves us with the problem of how to interpret such complicated sentences.

That QML allows such monsters as $\lozenge\lozenge\square\lozenge\lozenge\square\neg\square\lozenge\lozenge\lozenge\lozenge\varphi \rightarrow$ $\lozenge\square\lozenge\lozenge\square\square\lozenge\lozenge\lozenge\square\varphi$ gives the impression that QML is very strong. But, in fact, QML has severe limitations. Of course, some limitations will be due to the fact that QML is an extension of a *first*-order language. In so far as there are propositions, which must be expressed using plural quantification, or higher-order quantification, or infinitary quantifiers, we should not expect QML to overcome *these* limitations. So, for instance, "There are finitely many atoms" is a sentence that, arguably, cannot be formulated in the first-order predicate calculus,[10] but that can be formulated in the first-order predicate calculus plus the cardinality quantifier "there are finitely many", or in the second-order predicate calculus. But these kinds of limitations are irrelevant for our purposes; they arise not because of limitations of the new modal operators, but because of the limitations of the other parts of the language – the limitations of having only the two quantifiers $\exists$ and $\forall$, or the limitations of forbidding such quantification into predicate position. More to the point, there is a range of modal propositions that do not involve infinitary quantifiers or second-order logic yet which nevertheless cannot be formulated in QML. We now turn to these.

Expressive limitations of QML

We have seen that there are certain sentences of QML that are not easy to interpret. This is unfortunate, because we have not even begun to scratch the surface of our modal thought and talk. Indeed, there are a large number of intuitive and philosophical modal theses that do not seem to be expressible in QML. This is worrying. If we have to expand the conceptual resources of QML in order to express in a logical language the modal theses that we wish to express, we can expect the difficulties of interpretation to multiply.

We shall look here at three different kinds of modal theses that do not appear to be expressible using only the resources of QML.

Numerical quantification

"There are three different ways in which Joe could win his chess match." He could: (i) take advantage of his opponent's poor development by castling queenside and initiating a devastating attack on the kingside; (ii) take advantage of his opponent's awful pawn structure by simply doubling heavy pieces on the semi-open d file, attacking black's weak and backwards pawn; (iii) play Bxf7, giving checkmate. Instead, weak-minded fool that he is, he resigns. He resigns! And to think that there were three ways he could have won. But this simple modal truth is not expressible in QML.

The trouble is that QML merely gives us the means to say that certain things are possible or impossible. But sometimes we want to do more. Sometimes we want to *count* the ways in which something is possible, or say that there were many ways in which a certain thing was possible. What are we to do? We seem to be saying *something* true about the chess game when we say that there are three ways in which Joe could win. And if there were such things as possible worlds or possible ways in our ontology, we would have the necessary things in our ontology to make sense of such quantification. But given the mere resources of QML, there appears to be no way of formulating such sentences. Worse, it is very hard to see how QML could be extended in such a way that, without postulating such things as worlds or possibilities, we could express such numerical quantification at all.

Numerical quantification over possibilities is not restricted to things as trivial as chess matches. It may be a matter of some urgency to know that there are three ways in which we can escape from a burning building. It may be of great scientific interest to know that, given the initial conditions and the laws of nature, there are two ways in which a system can evolve. Yet none of these natural, important or scientific modal theses can be expressed using the resources of QML.

There could have been other things than there actually are
As things actually stand, I have exactly one brother. But I might have had a sister. Now, one way in which this possibility might have been true is if Susan down the road, or Jane across the street or even you, the reader, halfway across the world, had been my sister. However, this is not the natural way to think of such a possibility; rather, it is natural to think that this sister is not identical to anything that exists in the actual world. She is an object distinct from every actually existing thing; she is an object that is entirely new.

The possibility of entities distinct from every actually existing thing appears to be plausible. And thus we might say that there could have been things that don't actually exist. Unfortunately, there is no way to express this thought using QML. The sentence $\Diamond\exists x \neg Ex$ won't do. Translating it into English, this sentence says "It is possible that there be things that don't exist." But this is crazy! How could there be things that don't exist? *That* isn't what we were trying to say. Perhaps you think that the $\Diamond$ is in the wrong place. Perhaps it should occur *after* the existential quantifier: $\exists x \Diamond \neg Ex$. But this isn't right either. This says that there is something that might not have existed. This is true – I might not have existed, this computer might not have existed – but it isn't what we were trying to say. Again, QML fails us: it lacks the resources to express natural modal theses.

This is just the beginning. There are many sentences that, in possible worlds terms, compare the domains of different possible worlds. "There could have been fewer things than there actually are", "There couldn't have been a world which contained every possible object" and "There could have been a world that contained only the objects that don't actually exist" are all sensible, if esoteric, modal theses that cannot even be expressed in QML.[11]

Modalized comparatives

Your car could have been the same colour as my car actually is. As things actually are, my car is red and your car is green. But you could have painted your car red – so your car could have been the same colour as my car actually is. But how can we express this in QML? As a first attempt, we might try $\Diamond(Rab)$ – where a is the name for your car, b the name for mine and Rxy is "x is the same colour as y". But this isn't right. Sure, it is possible that my car could have been the same colour as your car. But that could be because it is possible that your car and my car could both have been yellow. But the original sentence says something stronger than this. What are we to do? There is no other place we can put the "$\Diamond$" within a sentence comparing the colours of our two cars and still get a formula that is well formed. QML simply lacks the resources to state the required sentence.

The sentence "My car could have been the same colour as your car actually is" is an example of a *modalized comparative*. Some other examples of modalized comparatives are: "My car can go faster than your car can", "I could have been taller than you actually are" and "An orange thing can resemble a red thing more closely than a green thing can." In all these cases, a modal operator interacts with a comparative in a way that cannot be understood simply in QML terms.

First-order quantification over possibilia

It is an expressive limitation of first-order languages that they cannot say that there are finitely many Fs. Few defenders of first-order languages respond by giving up on this concept. They argue that the concept *can* be expressed in a first-order language provided we allow ourselves to quantify over and refer to certain mathematical objects. For instance, if we accept the existence of the set of natural numbers ω, then first-order theorists point out that we can express "There are finitely many Fs" by the sentence "For some natural number n, there is a one-to-one correspondence from the set of Fs onto the set of numbers less than n." A drawback of such a course of action is that this sentence commits us to an ontology of mathematical objects. The advantage is that, if we accept this ontology, we are now able to express "There are finitely many Fs" without having to go beyond the conceptual apparatus of our familiar and well-understood first-order logic.[12]

Just as the postulation of sets and numbers enables us to express new truths about quantity in the familiar first-order predicate calculus, so the postulation of possible worlds and possible individuals enables us to express new truths about the modal in the familiar first-order predicate calculus. Indeed, a first-order language that is permitted to quantify over possibilia overcomes all the expressive limitations of QML noted above. Let us see what a typical first-order language that talks of possibilia looks like.[13]

As usual, our language (let us call it PWL for possible worlds language) will have the familiar existential and universal quantifiers plus the truth-functional connectives. It will also contain the usual supply of names and variables. Naturally, it will also contain predicates, but whereas in QML one-place predicates of English, such as "x is red", are treated as one-place predicates Fx, PWL treats them as *two*-place predicates Fxw. This is because, in the possible worlds framework, one object can have different properties at different worlds. One and the same object a can be green at the actual world but blue at some merely possible world. To accommodate such facts, we add an extra place to the predicate so as to make the world at which *a* has a particular property explicit. *Fxw* is to be read as saying "*x* is *F* at *w*".[14]

Like QML, PWL also contains a special predicate for identity: =. In our presentation, this predicate is still a two-place predicate. This reflects the fact that if two objects are identical at one world then they are identical at all worlds, and thus there is no need to make explicit the world at which the identity holds.[15]

Our language will also contain a predicate for exists, *E*, but whereas the existence predicate was a one-place predicate in QML, here the predicate is *two*-place: *Exw* is to be interpreted as saying that "*x* exists at *w*".

Our language will also contain two brand new items. First, it will contain the name *w**. This is to be thought of as the name for a particular possible world: the actual world. Secondly, it will contain the new one-place predicate *Wx*, which is to be read as "*x* is a possible world". That is *all* that is new about our language. In particular, it does not contain any new logical operators, such as □ and ◊.

As this is nothing more than a first-order language, the usual rules of well-formedness apply to this language and we can use what we know from the predicate calculus to put strings of symbols together to form grammatical sentences. Those familiar with first-order languages will be able to both recognize the strings $\forall x \exists y (Wy$ & $Exy)$, Eaw^*, and $\exists x (Wy$ & $Fax)$ & $\exists y (Wy$ & $\neg Fay)$ as wffs, and read these sentences.[16]

Numerical quantification revisited

Sentences such as "There are three ways in which Joe could win his chess match" count the possible ways in which a certain event could occur. Take this talk of *possible ways* at face value,[17] as a particular kind of entity: possible ways or possibilities. Where possible worlds are complete entities, making every single proposition true or false, a possible way is incomplete or partial: there are certain propositions whose truth-value it simply doesn't determine. In one of the possible ways that Joe wins his chess match, the one where he wins by playing Ne5, nothing is said as to whether or not unicorns exist or donkeys talk; these propositions are simply irrelevant. And we certainly don't want to count as *two* the ways in which Joe could win: (a) where he plays Ne5 and unicorns exist, and (b) where he plays Ne5 and unicorns don't exist. Identify such partial possibilities with *sets* of possible worlds: the possibility where Joe plays Ne5 will be the set of worlds at which Joe plays Ne5. We say that what is true at a possibility P is precisely what is true at all the worlds within the set. Armed with possibilities, we can treat such sentences in exactly the same way that the first-order predicate calculus treats any case of numerical quantification. The sentence "There are three ways in which Joe could win his chess match" becomes:

$\exists x \exists y \exists z (Px$ & Py & Py & Joe wins his chess match at x & Joe wins his chess match at y & Joe wins his chess match at z & $\neg x = y$ & $\neg x = z$ & $\neg y = z)$

where the predicate Px means "x is a possibility".

"There could have been other things than there actually are" revisited

We saw above that there are esoteric but meaningful modal theses that (in possible worlds terms) compare the sizes of the different domains of different worlds that are not expressible in QML. As illustration, let us see how PWL handles the sentences "There could have been more things than there actually are", "Only some of the objects that actually exist might have existed" and "There could have been a world containing only objects that don't actually exist."

"There could have been more things than there actually are" can be formalized as:

$$\exists z \{Wz\ \&[\forall x(Exw^* \rightarrow Exz)\ \&\ \exists y(\neg Eyw^*\ \&\ Eyz)]\}$$

Or, in words, "There is a world z such that anything that exists at the actual world exists at z; moreover, something exists at z that does not exist at the actual world."

"Only some of the objects that actually exist might have existed" can be formalized as:

$$\exists z \{Wz\ \&\ [\forall x(Exz \rightarrow Exw^*)\ \&\ \exists y(\neg Eyz\ \&\ Eyw^*)]\}$$

That is, "There is a world z such that anything that exists at z exists at the actual world; moreover, something actually exists at the actual world that does not exist at z."

Finally, "There could have been a world containing only objects that don't actually exist" can be formalized as:

$$\exists z[Wz \;\&\; \forall x(Exz \rightarrow \neg Exw^*)]$$

That is, "There is a possible world z such that anything that exists at z does not exist at the actual world."

Modalized comparatives revisited

The sentence "Your car could have been the same colour as my car actually is" can be understood as making a *crossworld comparison*. What we are doing is considering your car at some merely possible world, and comparing your car as it is at that merely possible world to my car as it is at the actual world. To express this thought, we will need to introduce the four-place predicate $Rxwyv$, which we take to mean "x at w is the same colour as y at v". Letting a be the name of my car, and b be the name of your car, we can now express the modalized comparative as $\exists w(Ww \;\&\; Rbwaw^*)$.[18]

It seems, then, that a language capable of quantifying and referring to possible worlds and possibilia is able to formulate plausible and natural modal theses that lie beyond the descriptive abilities of QML. Here we see some of the genuine work that possible worlds can do. Without an ontologically innocent way of expressing these theses, such quantification and reference to possibilia cannot be seen as a mere heuristic or a mere way of speaking. Those who take the kinds of modal theses discussed here seriously must either find another way of expressing these theses, or must start to take the ontology of possible worlds seriously.

Modal logic

A perplexing plethora

Developing a formal language capable of expressing a wide range of modal theses is only part of the logician's job. Logicians also wish to formalize the notion of a *valid inference*. Once a logical language has been set up, we want to formulate rules and axioms that, necessarily, never lead from truth to falsehood. In the first-order predicate calculus, rules such as conjunction elimination and existential introduction are relatively uncontroversial and there are few who dissent from the rules of classical logic.[19] It is not particularly hard for us to see that φ follows from φ & ψ, or that ∃*xFx* follows from *Fa*. By contrast, the situation in QML is obscure. The logical implications of sentences involving modal operators are far less clear and far more contentious.

True, some of the inferential properties of the modal operators are relatively clear. If something is true, then it is possible. Accordingly, adopting the axiom φ → ◇φ in a system of modal logic is uncontentious. Similarly, with a little thought, we can see that if *A* necessarily implies *B*, then if *A* is necessary so is *B*. So the sentence □(φ → ψ) → (□φ → □ψ) also seems an acceptable axiom.

Unfortunately, our intuitions now begin to fail us and we lose the ability to tell easily what we should take as axioms or theorems of our system. For instance, should □φ → □□φ be a theorem? Or φ → □◇φ? What about ◇◇□◇◇□¬□◇◇◇φ → ◇□◇◇□□◇◇◇□φ? We find it difficult to answer such questions, in part because it is not even clear whether we can make sense of such stacks of modal operators.[20] However, there are problems even with sentences that don't involve iterated modalities. For instance, does "Necessarily everything is *F*" entail "Everything is necessarily *F*"? In symbols, should □∀*xFx* → ∀*x*□*Fx* be accepted as an axiom of a quantified modal logic? There are no iterated modalities there yet our logical intuitions are very unclear.

Over the years, a vast number of competing modal systems were put forward, each purporting to be the correct system of modal inference. Indeed, there seemed to be more systems of modal logic than there were philosophers. But there was very little consensus and it was not clear how to resolve the situation. Such an impasse served only to support those who suspected that our intuitive grasp on the modal operators was in fact pathetically weak. How can one claim that the modal operators were well understood when almost any random collection of axioms seemed as good a system of modal inference as any other? How can one claim to have a firm grasp of the modal operators if one has no idea about the validity of the simplest modal arguments? Rather than putting modality on any kind of firm footing, the existence of a plurality of modal axiom systems merely served to fuel the suspicions of those who thought that modality was never a fit subject to study in the first place.

A semantics for modal logic might help us make progress on these questions. In the familiar non-modal quantificational logic, we could test our system of rules of inference against the semantics to make sure that the rules are sound and complete. If the system is *sound* then we have a guarantee that the rules and axioms of the system are not too strong: they cannot take us from a truth to a falsehood. Conversely, if the system is *complete*, we know that the rules don't miss anything out: no further rules or axioms are required for any valid inference to be carried out within the system.

With the discovery of possible worlds model theory for modal logic, logicians finally had a plausible formal semantics against which they could test their deductive systems for soundness and completeness. If we could show that a particular system was *unsound* then we would know that the system had to be rejected. If we could show that a system was incomplete, we would know that it was too weak and must be supplemented with further axioms. Accordingly, it seems as though results in possible worlds model theory could shed light on just what the correct system of modal inference should be.

But this line of thought must be treated with caution. After all, from one point of view, a formal semantics for a deductive system is nothing more than a piece of pure mathematics, and there is no immediate reason why pure mathematics should have conceptual or philosophical significance. It is true that, in the first-order and second-order cases, model theoretic results *are* generally taken to have conceptual significance: soundness is taken to show that our system can be trusted; completeness that our system needs no further rules or axioms. But one cannot derive a philosophical conclusion without philosophical premises. Without certain premises about the philosophical significance of model theory for first-order languages there will be no reason to regard results in model theory as having philosophical significance. Of course, these premises may be plausible or uncontentious. Indeed, in the first-order case, I believe that they are. But premises that are plausible in the first-order case may be contentious in the modal case. The mere fact that we use model-theoretic results to guide us in our choice of an axiom system in the first-order case is not, in itself, a reason for trusting the model theory in the modal case.

To find out why model-theoretic results are important in the first-order case, we will first look at the model theory for first-order languages, before outlining the model theory for QML. We shall see that the semantics for QML favours some systems of modal inference over others. Finally, we will examine whether the kinds of considerations that justify our use of model theory for first-order languages carry over to the modal case.

Argument and abstraction

One of the fundamental notions in logic is that of a valid argument. Roughly, an argument is valid if it is not possible for the premises to be true and the conclusion false. Now, it turns out that a wide class of arguments are valid simply in virtue of the meanings of *some* of the words that appear in the arguments. Consider the following arguments:

> Anything that is a man is mortal
> Socrates is a man
> _____
> Socrates is mortal

> Anything that is a whale is a mammal
> Moby is a whale
> _____
> Moby is a mammal

> Anything that is a dog is vicious
> Harry is a dog
> _____
> Harry is vicious

> Anything that is a boojum is a beejoom
> Tharrpx is a boojum
> _____
> Tharrpx is a beejoom

At least in the first three cases, we can see that the conclusion follows from the premises, for we can see that it is not possible for the premises to be true and the conclusion false. Note that we see this to be the case *independently* of whether or not we know the truth-value of the premises. For instance, in the third argument, many may dispute the premises. Perhaps they think that there are some dogs that are not vicious at all. Perhaps they think that Harry is not a dog. Perhaps they are sceptical of all knowledge of the external world. Whatever. The argument is still *valid* even if its premises are not true, for whatever the truth of the premises, it is still not *possible* for the premises to be true and the conclusion false. We can recognize the validity of an argument even if we do not know the truth of the premises. Indeed, we can see that the fourth argument is valid even though we may not know what the words in the argument mean, for we know that, as long as the words are of the right grammatical category (as long as "boojum" and "beejoom" are predicates and "Tharrpx" is a name), if the premises are true then the conclusion must be true also.

In a sense, this is an achievement. When I told you that an argument was valid if it was not possible for the premises to be true while the conclusion was false, you would not have thought that you would be capable of recognizing certain arguments as valid if you didn't know what some of the words in the argument meant. The point is that, in the cases above, the validity of all these arguments depends upon the meanings of only some of the words used in the argument. In each case, the predicates could have meant anything (provided they were still predicates) and the names could have meant anything (provided they were still names), and the argument would still be valid. By contrast, we cannot affect the meaning of the word "anything" and preserve the validity of the above arguments. Replacing "anything" by "something", for example, results in invalidity.

Finding a language capable of formalizing *every* valid inference is no easy project. But formalizing those arguments that are valid in virtue of the meanings of certain words is a more tractable project. Different choices of words lead to different logical systems: choosing just the truth-functional connectives leads to propositional logic; including the quantifiers and first-order variables leads to the first-order predicate calculus; including the identity symbol "=" leads to the first-order predicate calculus with identity; and permitting quantification into predicate position and adding second-order variables leads to second-order logic.

All the arguments given at the beginning of this section are formalized in the first-order predicate calculus in the following way:

$$\forall x(Fx \rightarrow Gx)$$
$$\frac{Fa}{Ga}$$

Note that *different* arguments in English are all formalized by exactly the same three lines. Moreover, we can see that, whatever *Fx*, *Gx* and *a* may mean, any argument that has this form will be valid, for any such argument owes its validity only to the meanings of the quantifier and the truth-functional connective →. The meaning of the other terms plays no real role in determining the argument's validity. Indeed, when we come to formalize the predicate calculus, the predicates *Fx*, *Gx* and so on are generally left *uninterpreted*. Only the quantifiers and the truth-functional connectives are thought of as having their meaning fixed once and for all. The interpretation of the predicates themselves is left open. Why? Because it is the task of the predicate calculus to study those arguments that owe their validity just to the meaning of the quantifiers and the truth-functional connectives. We can say that any argument that has the above form is valid just in virtue of the meanings of the quantifiers and the truth-functional connectives.

Model theory: the basics

Although it is easy see that any argument of the form

$$\forall x(Fx \rightarrow Gx)$$
$$\frac{Fa}{Ga}$$

is valid, one cannot always just look and see whether or not an argument of a certain form is valid. For instance, it is not intuitively obvious whether or not any argument of the form

$$\forall x \exists y \forall z [Rxy \rightarrow (\exists w Gzwy \vee \neg \forall u Guwz)]$$
$$\frac{\forall x \forall y \exists z [(Gxyy \,\&\, \neg Gxxz) \rightarrow \exists u(Rxz)]}{\forall x \forall y \exists z \forall u(Rxy \vee Gyzz \vee \neg Guzu)}$$

is valid. One way of dealing with this question is to use the formal rules of predicate calculus to try to construct a proof of the conclusion from the premises. But this approach is problematic. After all, what if the argument above is *invalid*? If it were, then we would *never* be able to prove the conclusion from the premises. But we cannot use the fact that *we* can't prove the conclusion from the premises as sufficient condition for the argument's being invalid. Maybe our failure to prove the conclusion is simply a consequence of our stupidity. We need firmer grounds than this for saying that the argument is invalid.

To see how to proceed, let us consider how we establish invalidity for a simple example. Consider the following argument form of the predicate calculus:

$$\frac{\forall x(Fx \lor Gx)}{\forall xFx \lor \forall xGx}$$

As a matter of fact, this argument is invalid: the conclusion doesn't follow from the premise. Moreover, we can *show* the argument's invalidity by describing a way in which the premises can be true and the conclusion is false. Such a way is given by Figure 2.1.

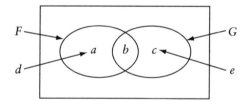

Figure 2.1

The big box represents a possible domain of quantification. The quantifiers of the language are understood to range over all and only the things in the box. As we can see, there are only three things in the box, a, b and c, so this box represents a particularly simple "possibility". The things that are in the left oval are to be thought of as those things that are F. So a and b are both F but c is not, and b and c are both G, but a is not. Moreover, according to the diagram, the name d refers to a and the name e refers to c. So Fd is true, but Gd is not, and Fe is false while Ge is true.

It is not hard to see that the premises of our argument are true in Figure 2.1 while the conclusion is false. According to the diagram, there is nothing that doesn't fall within at least one of the two ovals. Take anything you like in the big box, and it is F or it is G. So the sentence $\forall x(Fx \vee Gx)$ is true, according to the diagram.[21] However, it is not true that everything is F: c is not F. So $\forall xFx$ is false. Moreover, it is not true that everything is G: a is not G. So $\forall xGx$ is false. But if $\forall xFx$ and $\forall xGx$ are both false then, since the disjunction of two false sentences is itself false, $\forall xFx \vee \forall xGx$ must itself be false. So Figure 2.1 represents a possible situation where the premise of the argument is true and the conclusion of the argument is false. So the argument is invalid.

We worked out that the argument was invalid without knowing what the predicates Fx and Gx mean. In Figure 2.1, nothing is assumed about what these predicates mean. We do not have to take a stance on the meaning of these predicates to recognize that the diagram represents a situation where the premises are true and the conclusion is false. This is good news indeed. As we saw, in the predicate calculus we were interested in precisely those arguments that were valid solely in virtue of the meanings of the logical constants of the language. In such a context, we *don't* want to make any substantive assumptions about the meanings of the predicates.

Now, it may be that, under a certain choice of the meanings of the predicates, the above argument becomes valid. Suppose we took Fx to mean "x is identical to itself", and Gx to mean "x is green". Under such a choice of predicates, the argument would come out valid, for the conclusion would have to be true. Since no matter how the world is everything *is* identical to itself, the first disjunct is always true. However, in so far as we are formalizing the notion of valid inference for the predicate calculus, we actually *want* our models to be indifferent to this. We are interested only in those inferences that owe their validity to the meaning of the logical constants, *not* to the meanings of the basic predicates. Accordingly, we want our models to make minimal assumptions about the meanings of the predicates. Indeed, in general, all that the models assume about the meaning of the predicate Fx is that some, none or all are F.

Models for the predicate calculus are essentially just mathematical versions of diagrams. The models contain a set of objects, D, that forms the domain of quantification, or the "universe", of the model. In Figure 2.1, D was nothing more than the set of objects {a, b, c}. The models also tell us which things are F and which things are G. In Figure 2.1, the things that were F were a and b, and the things that were G were b and c. More formally, we say that the model assigns the set {a, b} to the predicate F and the set {b, c} to the predicate G.

Figure 2.1 dealt only with one-place predicates. For two- or higher-place predicates, using such diagrams begins to be a little clumsy. While it may make sense to ask "According to the model, which are the things that are F?", it doesn't make much sense to ask "According to the model, which are the things that are R?" This is like asking what the "taller than" things are. When dealing with two-place predicates, the correct question to ask is "Which are the *pairs* of things, <a, b>, such that a bears R to b?" Accordingly, in this case, what we really want the model to do is assign a set of *pairs* of objects (of the domain of the model) to the predicate R. If a model assigns <a, b> to the predicate R, we can think of the model as saying that a does bear R to b. If <a, b> is not assigned to the predicate R by the model, we can think of the model as saying that a does not bear R to b. Similarly, when it comes to modelling a three-place predicate H, the model needs to tell us which *triples* of objects belong to the predicate H.

First-order languages contain names as well as predicates. Just as our model has to tell us which predicates of our formal language are satisfied by which n-tuples, so it has to tell us which names of our language refer to which objects. Accordingly, our model must associate with each name in our formal language some element of D.[22] In Figure 2.1, the idea was represented by connecting arrows from each name to an element in the domain.

Formally, we say that a model is an ordered pair <D, val>, where D is a set of entities that is the domain of the model, and val is a function that maps names onto elements of D, one-place predicates onto subsets of D, two-place predicates onto subsets of D^2, three-place predicates onto subsets of D^3 and so on.[23] There is no reason for putting D before val. It would not have made any difference to choose our models to be of the form <val, D>. Nor is there any reason why we have chosen *one* function, val, rather than many functions f_0 (which maps names onto elements of D), f_1 (which maps one-place predicates onto subsets of D), f_2 (which maps two-place predicates onto subsets of D^2), f_3 (which maps three-place predicates onto subsets of D^3) and so on, and let our models be ω-tuples of the form $<D, f_1, f_2, f_3, \ldots>$. When we use mathematics to capture a concept, there are often many different ways to do it and the preferred mathematical representation often has some arbitrary features.

As an illustration, we present the model corresponding mathematically to Figure 2.1. In this case,

$$M = <D, \text{val}>$$

where

$$
\begin{aligned}
D &= \{a, b, c\} \\
\text{val}(F) &= \{a, b\} \\
\text{val}(G) &= \{b, c\} \\
\text{val}(d) &= a \\
\text{val}(e) &= c
\end{aligned}
$$

It is relatively straightforward to tell which sentences are true in a model and which sentences are false. Since b is in both val(G) and val(F), according to this model there is something that is both G and F. So the sentence $\exists x(Gx \ \& \ Fx)$ is true in the model. Since everything is either in val(G) or val(F) we can see that the sentence $\forall x(Fx \lor Gx)$ is true. Since everything that is not in val(G) is in val(F) we can see that the sentence $\forall x(\neg Gx \to Fx)$ is true. And so on. With a little practice, most people can tell whether or not a particular sentence is true or false in a particular model. The relation "φ is true in M" is of central importance in logic and we introduce a special symbol for it: ⊨.

Although it may be easy to see intuitively when $M ⊨ φ$, the logician wants a mathematical definition of this relation. Accordingly, the logician goes on to define $M ⊨ φ$ for an arbitrary model M and sentence φ using an inductive process. Informally, the model first tells us what happens at the base level: which things satisfy which predicates; which names refer to which individuals; what the domain of quantification is. This information fixes certain semantic truths about the simplest parts of the language under question and, by a process of induction, semantic truths about more complex parts of the language are defined in terms of the semantic truths at the simpler levels. An example of such an inductive process at its simplest is the inductive clause for sentences whose main connective is the conjunction &:

$$M \vDash \varphi \ \& \ \psi \text{ iff } M \vDash \varphi \text{ and } M \vDash \psi$$

In propositional logic, all the inductive clauses for $\vDash$ were as simple as this. However, in first-order predicate logic things are not quite so simple and it turns out that, in order to define truth in a model the relation "φ is satisfied by $<a_1, \ldots, a_n>$" in a model must be inductively defined first. Satisfaction in a model and truth in a model are closely related notions and, usually, the same symbol is used for both. Thus we write $M \vDash \varphi <a_1, \ldots, a_n>$ symbolizes "φ is satisfied by $<a_1, \ldots, a_n>$ in M".

To illustrate the idea, consider Figure 2.1 again. The formula Fx is not true or false in the diagram. Rather, certain things satisfy or fail to satisfy this formula. For example, a satisfies Fx, and b satisfies Fx, but c does not. The diagram tells us directly which objects or ordered n-tuples of objects[24] satisfy which basic predicates of the language. Using this information, we can then inductively define which objects satisfy which complex predicates. Included in such an inductive definition will be clauses such as:

$Fx \ \& \ Gx$ is satisfied by a in M *iff* Fx is satisfied by a in M and Gx is satisfied by a in M.

Or, using the notation above,

$$M \vDash Fx \ \& \ Gx <a> \text{ iff } M \vDash Fx <a> \text{ and } M \vDash Gx <a>$$

The formal pay-off for concentrating on satisfaction is that it gives us a straightforward way of writing inductive clauses for the quantifiers. Thus, where φ has n free variables, we can say:

$$M \vDash \forall x_n \varphi(x_1, \ldots, x_n) <a_1, \ldots, a_{n-1}> \text{ iff, for all } z \text{ in } D,$$
$$M \vDash \varphi(x_1, \ldots, x_n) <a_1, \ldots, a_{n-1}, z>$$

Note that the formula $\forall x_n \varphi(x_1, \ldots, x_n)$ is satisfied by sequences containing one fewer member than those that satisfy $\varphi(x_1, \ldots, x_n)$; this is because it contains one fewer free variable.[25]

When our φ contains only one free variable, an application of the above clause yields:

$$M \vDash \forall x \varphi(x) <> \text{ iff, for all } z \text{ in } D, M \vDash \varphi(x) <z>$$

This looks slightly strange: the right-hand side contains a "sequence" with only one member! This is nothing more than a technicality. Just to keep the clauses uniform, we will write down clauses like $M \vDash \varphi(x) <z>$, but take this to mean nothing more than that z satisfies φx in M. The left-hand side contains a formula being satisfied by an empty sequence, but this just codes the fact that the formula in question is a closed formula, a sentence, and thus that it is true or false *simpliciter* in the model, rather than a predicate with free variables, which is true or false *of* certain objects or n-tuples in the model. In this way, the truth of certain complex sentences can be understood as nothing more than a special case of satisfaction: the case where the sentence is satisfied by the empty sequence.

Once truth in a model has been mathematically defined, a formal definition of validity is not far away. Whenever there is a model that makes the premises of an argument true and the conclusion of an argument false, then that argument is invalid. Nobody has any difficulty in seeing that the model given by Figure 2.1 shows that the argument is invalid. It does this because it represents a way in which the premises of the argument could be true and the conclusion false. The domain of the model might have been the things in D; the extension of F might have been b and c; the extension of G might have been a and b. Since a valid argument is one that cannot have true premises and a false conclusion, we see that the existence of such a model is sufficient to make the argument form invalid.

The converse – that if an argument is invalid then there is a model that makes the premises of the argument true and the conclusion false – is less clear. As a matter of fact, there are excellent technical reasons for believing this to be true.[26] Intuitively, there are so many different models one could construct, models that have domains of any arbitrary infinite cardinality, from which *any* arbitrary subset may be the extension of a one-place predicate, that it seems plausible that our models are rich enough to represent all the relevant possible ways in which the sentences of the predicate calculus could be true.

But if it is a necessary and sufficient condition of an argument form's being invalid that there be a model where the premises are true and the conclusion is false, then that means that we can use models to *define* a precise, mathematical concept of validity, rather than leaving this concept primitive and intuitive. Accordingly, logicians *define* validity for the first-order predicate calculus in the following way:

> An argument is valid iff every model that makes the premises of the argument true also makes the conclusion of the argument true.

Model theory for modal languages: an intuitive heuristic

Before proceeding to a more formal presentation of model theory for QML, we examine an heuristic for thinking about its models. The ideas embodied in Figure 2.2 will need modification later, but it will give us an intuitive basis for the formal ideas that follow.

In Figure 2.2, the big box can be thought of as the set of all possible worlds.[27] Each of the three shaded circles represents a

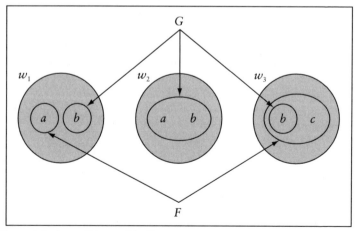

Figure 2.2 A possible worlds diagram

particular possible world. Each of these possible worlds is rather like a model for the predicate calculus and they make sentences true or false in a way familiar from the the first-order predicate calculus. The leftmost world, w_1, contains two elements: a, which is F but not G, and b, which is G but not F. Similarly, w_2 contains the same two elements, a and b, both of which are G here. Note that nothing is F at w_2. The rightmost world again contains two elements, this time b and c, both of which are F, but only b is G.

For non-modal sentences, that is, sentences that do not contain $\Box$ or $\Diamond$, determining which sentences are true or false at a world is just the same as determining which sentences are true or false in a model in the first-order predicate calculus. To work out whether or not a modal sentence is true or false in the model, we just have to see which non-modal sentences are true at the various worlds.

The central idea in possible worlds semantics is that necessity claims are true if they are true at all possible worlds, and possibility claims are true if they are true at some possible world. In other words, the modal operators are treated as *quantifiers*. It is not hard to see intuitively that the sentence $\Box\exists x Gx$ is true in Figure 2.2. Why? Because $\exists x Gx$ is true at every single world in the model. By contrast, the sentence $\Box\exists x Fx$ is not true in Figure 2.2. Why? Since $\exists x Fx$ is *not* true at w_2, $\exists x Fx$ is not true at all worlds. One can also see that the sentence $\exists x \Box Gx$ (There is something that is necessarily G) is true in Figure 2.2. Look at b. In every single world it is true of b that it falls under the extension of the predicate G. Accordingly, at every world, b satisfies Gx. By the quantificational treatment of $\Box$, this amounts to: necessarily, b satisfies Gx. So, by the meaning of $\exists$, it follows that $\exists x \Box Gx$ is true in the model shown in Figure 2.2. Although what follows is technical, it is little more than the formalization of the notion of a possible world and a formalization of the processes we go through to recognize truth or falsehood in such possible world models.

Model theory for modal languages in six easy pieces

1. $<W, ?>$

Just as with the first-order predicate calculus, we shall want our models to assign truth-values to the sentences of our quantified modal languages in a way that is consonant with the logical constants of the language. Our models have to have enough structure so that, as before, we can inductively define a relation $M \vDash \varphi$,[28] where now φ is a sentence in the language of QML. Whereas models for the predicate calculus were ordered pairs, we suppose that models for QML consist of n-tuples and we now work out what should appear in the various places of the n-tuple by stages.

The basic idea in possible worlds semantics is to treat necessity as truth at *all* possible worlds and possibility as truth at *some* possible world. This idea promises to provide a model theory that will be similar to the familiar model theory for predicate languages, for the two modal operators $\square$ and $\lozenge$ are essentially both being treated as nothing more than quantifiers: the former universal, the latter existential. True, these are quantifiers over a new and special kind of object – a possible world – but they are still quantifiers for all that.

In the case of the first-order predicate calculus we needed a set D for the domain of the universal and existential quantifiers. Since $\square$ and $\lozenge$ are treated as quantifiers over possible worlds, our models must contain a set W that is going to count as the domain of these quantifiers. W is a set of objects that, intuitively, can be thought of as the *set of all possible worlds*.

We now at least know what the first place in our n-tuple is: it is the set W. Models for QML have the form $<W, ?>$, where the question marks leave open whatever further structure we may need to add to our models.

2. $<W, ?, w>$

Models assign truth-values to sentences in a way that can be defined by an inductive process. The truth- (or satisfaction-) conditions of complex formulas depend on the truth- (or satisfaction-) conditions of the simpler parts of the formulas. Now, models for the predicate calculus could be thought of as representing a way in which the sentences of the language could come true. Accordingly, it made sense for us to talk of sentences being true or false *simpliciter* in a particular model. However, the question as to whether or not a particular sentence is true or false *simpliciter* doesn't yet make sense in a possible worlds model. Consider again Figure 2.2. Is $\exists x F x$ true or false in this diagram? The right answer is "It depends." At w_1 and w_3, the sentence is true, but at w_2 the sentence is false. In possible worlds semantics, do not ask whether a sentence is true *simpliciter* in a model; rather, ask whether it is true *at world w* in a model.

We might respond to this hitch by giving up on an inductive definition of the two-place relation $<W, ?> \vDash \varphi$, replacing it instead by an inductive definition of the *three*-place relation $<W, ?> \vDash_w \varphi$,[29] where w is a world in W. This is a perfectly legitimate way to proceed and many presentations of possible worlds semantics take this route. However, for technical reasons, we prefer to retain the idea that $\vDash$ is essentially a two-place relation between models and sentences. Instead of writing the world variable w as a subscript on the $\vDash$, we put the world variable within the tuple itself, and write $<W, ?, w> \vDash \varphi$ instead.[30] We will pronounce this relation "φ is true in $<W, ?, w>$ at w". As an illustration of this idea with respect to Figure 2.2, it should be clear that

$$<W, ?, w_1> \vDash \exists x Fx$$

while

$$<W, ?, w_2> \vDash \neg\exists x Fx$$

and

$$<W, ?, w_3> \vDash \exists x Fx$$

3. $<W, w^*, ?, w>$

By letting our models be of the form $<W, ?, w>$ we make room for the notion of truth at an arbitrary world. However, models are supposed to assign truth-values to sentences of a language in a way that respects the meanings of the logical constants of the language. What is the link between this relativized notion of truth, truth at a world, and *real* truth, truth *simpliciter*? Happily, from a possible worlds point of view, there is a clear and obvious connection between truth at a world and truth *simpliciter*, for truth *simpliciter* can be thought of as a special case of truth at a world: it is just a matter of what is true *at the actual world*.

Look again at the possible worlds diagram in Figure 2.2. Suppose I modified this diagram by colouring one of the worlds, say w_2, and told you that, in this picture, w_2 represents the actual world. Accordingly, when assessing what is actually true or false in this modified diagram, you should see what is true or false at w_2. In this way, we can again talk of sentences being true or false in such modified diagrams. $\exists xFx$ is *not* true in this coloured diagram, because $\exists xFx$ is not true at w_2. $\exists xGx$ is true in this coloured diagram, because $\exists xGx$ is true at w_2.[31]

Colouring a world in our diagram is merely a device for marking out a privileged world in the model, and instructing you to assess truth or falsehood in the model from the point of view of that particular world. To carry out this idea in model theory, we let our models for QML contain a place in the tuple for a world in W, a world distinguished by the model as representing actuality. We do this by picking out one particular world from W, call it w^*, and add this world to our tuple. A sentence is true in a model iff the sentence is true at w^* in the model. Models for QML therefore have the form $<W, w^*, ?, w>$, where $w^* \in W$. Truth *simpliciter* in a model will be understood as truth at the actual world in a model: truth at w^*. Since truth at an arbitrary world in a model w is modelled as truth at $<W, w^*, ?, w>$, we can write $<W, w^*, ?, w^*> \vDash \varphi$ as "φ is true in $<W, w^*, ?, w^*>$" as well as "φ is true at w^* in $<W, w^*, ?, w^*>$". When we come to define validity, it will be defined in terms of truth in a model, rather than truth at an arbitrary w in the model. This is just a sign that, when defining validity, we restrict our attention to models of the form $<W, w^*, ?, w^*>$.

4. $<W, w^*, R, ?, w>$

Model theory for modal languages treats necessity and possibility as a kind of quantifier over possible worlds. In Figure 2.2, we concluded that $\square\exists xGx$ was true at w_2 because $\exists xGx$ was true at *all* the worlds. However, this is a simplification of what actually happens in the model theory for QML. In model theory, the notion of necessity is treated as a *restricted* universal quantifier and we introduce a new relation R, the accessibility relation, which holds between different possible worlds. We say that $\square\varphi$ is true at w iff φ is true at all worlds w' that are *accessible* to w.

In the context of absolute necessity, the notion of *accessibility* is not a natural idea. To get some intuitive grasp of the nature of accessibility, consider the related notions of *physical* possibility and *physical* necessity. These two concepts quite clearly cannot be modelled by universal and existential quantification over all worlds. It is not physically possible that matter travel faster than light, but this is *metaphysically* possible. Accordingly, a model theory that treated "It is physically possible that φ" as true at w precisely if there is (unrestrictedly) some world w' at which φ is true, would just misrepresent the facts about physical possibility: the physically possible would be conflated with the metaphysically possible.

One response might be to abandon the quantificational approach to physical possibility and necessity altogether. But a less radical approach would be to retain the central quantificational idea while *restricting* the quantifier. True, there are worlds at which matter travels faster than light. But now, if L is the set of laws that hold at the actual world, there is no world where (i) the set of laws L hold and (ii) matter travels faster than light. In general, something is physically necessary (possible) iff it is true at all (some) worlds that obey the same laws.[32]

This idea can be put quite generally:

For any world w, φ is physically possible at w iff there is some world w' that obeys the same laws as w, and φ is true at w'.

For any world w, φ is physically necessary at w iff for all worlds w' that obey the same laws as w, φ is true at w'.

"w' obeys the same laws as w" is an example of a natural accessibility relation that here restricts the scope of the quantifiers. We would adopt such an accessibility relation in a semantics for a system that modelled the notions of *physical* possibility and necessity. Note that the relation is *not* universal:[33] there are different possible worlds that do not obey the same laws.

Since we want our model theory to be as flexible as possible, we will assume very little about the nature of the accessibility relation and treat it in a highly general form. In particular, note that although □ is now being treated as truth at all accessible worlds, it is quite open to us to let the accessibility relation be the universal relation, so that no generality is lost by introducing this relation.

We are now ready to fill in another place in our *n*-tuple. The model theory will treat □*P* as true at *w* iff *P* is true at all worlds *w'* that are *accessible* to *w*. Accordingly, our models need to include the accessibility relation in their structure. Thus we take our models to be of the form <*W, w*, R, ?, w*>, where *R* is a two-place *relation* on the elements of *w*.

Although we may want our model theory to be as flexible as possible, in presentations of modal logic it is typical to restrict ourselves to models where the accessibility relation is *reflexive*: that is, for any world *w* in the model, *wRw* in the model. In other words, every world can "see" itself. Restricting our attention to models where the accessibility relation is reflexive has interesting consequences for our notion of validity, as we shall see.

5. <*W, w*, R, D, d, ?, w*>

Referring back to Figure 2.2, we see that different objects exist at different worlds. ∃*xFx* is true at w_1 because *a* exists at w_1 and is *F* there. ∃*xFx* is false at w_2 because there is nothing that exists at w_2 that is *F*. Note that, even though there is something that exists at w_3 that *is* *F* there – namely *c* – this has nothing at all to do with the fact that, at w_2, there is nothing that is *F*. Only the things that exist at w_2 are relevant to whether or not an existential sentence is true at w_2. (This treatment of the quantifiers – the fact that they are restricted to the domain of different worlds – will become significant in Chapter 4.) Our models for QML will have to allow for the fact that, at different worlds, the quantifiers can range over different objects. This is done in two steps.

We first introduce a domain *D*, which intuitively can be thought of as the set of all possible objects, as the fourth place in our model. Now our models have the form <*W, w*, R, D, ?, w*>. In Figure 2.2, set *D* was nothing more than {*a, b, c*}. This gives us a set of possible individuals but it does not yet give us the notion of different objects existing at different worlds. For this, we also introduce a *function d*, which associates a subset of *D* with each element of *W*. In Figure 2.2, $d(w_1) = \{a, b\}$, $d(w_2) = \{a, b\}$ and $d(w_3) = \{b, c\}$. Now we can say that a quantified formula, such as ∃*xφx*, will be true in a model <*W, w*, R, D, d, ?, w*> iff there is some element *a* of *d(w)* such that <*a*> satisfies φ*x* at *w*.

6. $<W, w^*, R, D, d, val, w>$

Finally we come to val; as with the predicate calculus, this is a function that maps various parts of QML onto various structures defined on our set-theoretic n-tuple.

In the case of names, val behaves here in precisely the same way it behaved in the predicate calculus case: val(a) is an element of D. However, even here, philosophical issues about naming can influence the way in which we wish to define val. D is the set of all *possible* objects. Formal systems are supposed to be some kind of approximation to our *actual* languages. Is it plausible to think that, in our language, we have *names*, as opposed to descriptions, for merely possible objects? If so, what on earth do these names denote? I have no worries about supposing that the name "Joseph Melia" denotes me, and the name "Tony Blair" denotes the British prime minister. But the *denoting* relation has existential implications: if a denotes b then, trivially, there is something that the name denotes. So if we don't want to believe in merely possible objects, our names can only denote actual entities.

This worry might prompt us to modify the model theory so that the referents of the names of the formal language under investigation are drawn only from entities that exist at w^*, the actual world. But this proposal is also not without its drawbacks. For instance, intuitively we might think that, although Sherlock Holmes doesn't actually exist, he *might* have existed. We might try to represent this possibility in QML by writing $\Diamond Ea$. Of course, since the sentence Ea occurs within the scope of a possibility operator, $\Diamond Ea$ doesn't commit us to there being any such thing as a. However, if in our semantics we insist that names can only refer to things that exist at w^*, we will not be able to model such statements. Since, as a matter of fact, Sherlock Holmes *doesn't* actually exist, the name a has no denotation in w^*. So if we follow this restriction, there is no world where Ea is true, and thus $\Diamond Ea$ does not come out as true at w^*. With these worries in mind, we follow the logician's usual approach of letting val(a) be *any* object from D, the set of all possible objects.

So much for names. What about the predicates of our language? Whereas in the predicate calculus, val had only to tell us once and for all which things were G, which things were F, which pairs of things satisfied the R relation and so on, for QML val needs to tell us which things are *G at which worlds*. Look again at Figure 2.2. Notice that the extension of *G* is different at different worlds. At w_1 and w_3 just *b* falls under *G*. At w_2, both *a* and *b* fall under its extension. So given the domain *D* of possible objects {*a*, *b*, *c*} we cannot simply let the extension of *G* be a subset of *D*.

This complication is handled by taking val(*G*) to be a function that associates a subset of *D* with each world in *W*. So, for example, in Figure 2.2, val(*G*) maps w_1 to {*b*}, w_2 to {*a*, *b*} and w_3 to {*b*}; val(*F*) maps w_1 to {*a*}, w_2 to { } and w_3 to {*b*, *c*}. For a two-place predicate *R*, val(*R*) is a function from *W* to ordered pairs of *D*. For a three-place predicate *H*, val(*H*) is a function from *W* to ordered triples of *D*. And so on. Although the mathematical description is a little abstract, all that is happening is that these mappings encode information as to which objects (or *n*-tuples) satisfy which predicates at which worlds.

Validity

We now have enough structure in <*W*, w^*, *R*, *D*, *d*, val, *w*> to define truth-in-a-model, much as it was defined in the first-order predicate calculus. As in the first-order case, the notion of satisfaction-in-a-model is defined first. Analogously to the first-order case, our models have just enough structure to allow us to give the inductive steps, telling us which *n*-tuples of objects from *D* satisfy which formulas at which worlds. So, for instance, we say that:

<*W*, w^*, *R*, *D*, *d*, val, *w*> ⊨ *Fx* <*a*> iff val(*F*) maps *w* to a subset of *D* that includes *a*.

(This is nothing more than a formal way of saying "In the model, object *a* is *F* at *w*.") In the case of a two-place atomic predicate, we say that:

<*W*, w^*, *R*, *D*, *d*, val, *w*> ⊨ *Rxy* <*a*, *b*> iff val(*R*) maps *w* to a subset of ordered pairs of *D* that includes the pair <*a*, *b*>.

(Again, this is nothing more than a formal way of saying "In the model, *a* bears *R* to *b* at *w*.") Similar definitions hold for *n*-place atomic predicates.

With val determining what n-tuples satisfy what formulas in the atomic case, the route is now clear to give the inductive definitions of satisfaction. For the truth-functional connectives, life is exactly the same as in the first-order predicate calculus. Thus,

$<W, w^*, R, D, d, \text{val}, w> \vDash \neg\varphi <a_1, \ldots, a_n>$ iff it is not the case that $<W, w^*, R, D, d, \text{val}, w> \vDash \varphi <a_1, \ldots, a_n>$

and similar clauses hold for the other truth-functional connectives.[34]

For the existential quantifier, the following clauses are given

$<W, w^*, R, D, d, \text{val}, w> \vDash \exists x\varphi(x_1, \ldots, x_n, x) <a_1, \ldots, a_n>$
iff, for some a in the domain of w, $<W, w^*, R, D, d, \text{val}, w>$
$\vDash \varphi(x_1, \ldots, x_n, x) <a_1, \ldots, a_n, a>$

A similar clause is given for the universal quantifier. Again, this is familiar from the first-order predicate calculus but note that, in this case, the quantifiers are restricted to objects that exist at the world under consideration. The idea is that, when considering a quantified sentence from the point of view of a world w, we should restrict the domain of quantification to the things that actually exist at w.

The inductive clause for $\square$ is

$<W, w^*, R, D, d, \text{val}, w> \vDash \square \varphi(x_1, \ldots, x_n) <a_1, \ldots, a_n>$ iff
$<W, w^*, R, D, d, \text{val}, w'> \vDash \varphi(x_1, \ldots, x_n) <a_1, \ldots, a_n>$ for all
worlds w' such that wRw'.

As before, a closed sentence is true in a model precisely when it is satisfied by the empty sequence, false otherwise. In this way, models assign truth-values to all the sentences of QML.

We might now define a valid argument as one for which there is no model where the premises are true and the conclusion false, but it is at this point that the model theory becomes a little more subtle. It turns out that which sentences are valid depends on certain formal constraints that we put upon the accessibility relation. For instance, it turns out that the sentence $\varphi \rightarrow \Diamond\varphi$ is true in all models with a reflexive accessibility relation.

Consider a model $M = <W, w^*, R, D, d, \text{val}, w>$, where R is reflexive. Apart from the constraint that R is reflexive, this model is arbitrary. Now, either $<W, w^*, R, D, d, \text{val}, w> \vDash \varphi$ or $<W, w^*, R, D, d, \text{val}, w> \vDash \neg\varphi$. If the latter then, just by the truth-table for $\rightarrow$, $<W, w^*, R, D, d, \text{val}, w> \vDash \varphi \rightarrow \Diamond\varphi$, because, by the truth-table of $\rightarrow$, a model that makes φ false will make $\varphi \rightarrow \psi$ true, for *any* ψ. On the other hand, if $<W, w^*, R, D, d, \text{val}, w> \vDash \varphi$ then, since our model is reflexive, there is a world w', namely w itself, such that wRw' and $<W, w^*, R, D, d, \text{val}, w'> \vDash \varphi$. But, by the inductive definition of truth in a model for $\Diamond\varphi$, this means that $<W, w^*, R, D, d, \text{val}, w> \vDash \Diamond\varphi$. So, again, $<W, w^*, R, D, d, \text{val}, w> \vDash \varphi \rightarrow \Diamond\varphi$. Since this is true for an arbitrary model with a reflexive accessibility relation, it follows that *any* model with a reflexive accessibility relation makes $\varphi \rightarrow \Diamond\varphi$ true.

The sentence $\varphi \rightarrow \Diamond\varphi$ is a very plausible truth about modality. After all, if something is true, then it is surely possible. Surely, any logic that deserves to be called a logic of *modality* would accept such an axiom. But now it turns out that, if we allow models where the accessibility relation is not reflexive, then there are models where the sentence comes out as *false*. This means that if we choose to define validity as truth in *all* models, including models where the accessibility relation is not reflexive, the sentence $\varphi \rightarrow \Diamond\varphi$ will not be valid. But the axioms of our logical system *should* be valid!

The answer to this problem is simple: change the definition of a model for QML. Let models for QML be n-tuples of the form $<W, w^*, R, D, d, \text{val}, w>$ *where R is reflexive*. Now with this definition in place, $\varphi \rightarrow \Diamond\varphi$ will be true in all models and there is no objection to taking it as an axiom.

Life was easier in the model theory for predicate calculus; we didn't have to restrict ourselves to a special set of n-tuples. But, just as there are choices over which deductive system we should choose, so there are choices to make about what the semantics for modal logic should be, even within the possible worlds framework. In particular, there are choices to be made over the correct set of structures over which validity should be defined. In this case, we find ourselves ruling out n-tuples where the accessibility relation is not symmetric. But it is exactly here that we find another bonus of the possible worlds framework. It seemed right to restrict our attention to models that validate the sentence $\varphi \rightarrow \Diamond\varphi$ because it seemed right to take this sentence as an axiom. But, as we saw, there are many sentences whose truth or falsity we are unable to tell. Should $\Box\varphi \to \Box\Box\varphi$ be an axiom? Or $\Diamond\varphi \to \Box\Diamond\varphi$? Instead of using pre-theoretic intuitions about the intuitive validity of modal sentences to guide us in our definition of validity and our choice of a possible worlds semantics, why not reverse the process? That is, why not use our intuitions about possible worlds to guide us in our choice of the correct set of structures over which validity should be defined, and use the definition of validity to discover the correct system of modal logic? After all, if we take the possible worlds picture seriously, and treat $\Diamond$ and $\Box$ and quantifiers over worlds then, intuitively, *any* world should be accessible to any other. After all, the core Leibnizian intuition is that metaphysical necessity is truth at *all* possible worlds. This *all* is an unrestricted all: be there a single world, no matter how distant, remote or unlikely, at which φ fails, then φ is not necessary. In other words, the accessibility relation should be *universal*: when modelling metaphysical necessity, all worlds are accessible to other worlds. But to say that the accessibility relation is universal is to put certain constraints upon the class of models over which validity is to be defined. Just as before, where we restricted our attention to models where every world was accessible to itself, we might now claim that, on reflection on the possible worlds picture, we should further restrict our attention to models where every world is accessible to every other.[35]

It turns out that by taking this step we can discover the valid formulas. The formula $\Box\varphi \to \Box\Box\varphi$ is true in all models where every world is accessible to every other, and the formula $\Diamond\varphi \to \Box\Diamond\varphi$ is true in all models where every world is accessible to every other. Even more complicated formulas, containing stacks of iterated modal operators, can be seen to be valid or invalid in the relevant set of models. Questions about validity and the truth of complex formulas that couldn't be answered in the old framework can now be answered – but at a price. We only seem to get these answers if we take the possible worlds picture seriously. The intuition that all the worlds should be accessible from each other comes from reflecting on the possible worlds picture of modality. We cannot use advances and results from this picture, advances and results that do not seem to be obtainable by other methods, and then turn around and dismiss it as *merely* a heuristic, for we are now using the framework to do genuine and indispensable work in guiding our opinions about modal issues. One who believes that possible worlds truly reflect the structure of modal reality, and that $\Box$ and $\Diamond$ are truly to be understood in a quantificational way, can justify his use of possible worlds semantics in the search for the correct system of modal inference. But if one doesn't accept these things, then what justification can one have for using the framework to justify new beliefs about modality?

The philosophy of model theory

Our intuitive motivation for taking models for modal logic to be n-tuples of the form $<W, w^*, R, D, d, \text{val}, w>$ and for presenting our definition of truth-in-a-model was entirely in terms of the possible worlds picture. Nonetheless, the model theory itself does not commit us to possible worlds or possibilia. As a piece of pure mathematics, the model commits us to the existence of sets, and whatever things we take W, w^* and D to be. However, as a piece of pure mathematics, there is absolutely no reason to think that the elements of W *are* possible worlds, or that the elements of D *are* possible objects. Indeed, the elements of W and D could be tables and chairs, fish and chips, shoes and socks or any arbitrary collection of things that we like. Indeed, they could be nothing more than pure sets themselves. As long as there are *some* things that appear within W and D, the inductive definition of truth-in-a-model can still go ahead. This looks like great news, for it now looks as if we have the best of both worlds; we can help ourselves to the model-theoretic semantics for modal logic without having to believe in anything as preposterous as a plurality of possible worlds and possibilia, and without getting into any of the infuriating and interminable metaphysical problems that such a metaphysics presents.

This impression is false. If we wish to treat possible worlds model theory as anything more than a clever mathematical game, if we want to use the semantics to help us understand and illuminate our modal concepts, if the semantics is to be a guide to the logical properties of modal languages, and if the formal definition of validity is to have anything to do with our intuitive conception of validity, then we need some kind of justification of our choice of semantics. After all, suppose that, in the interests of living a life free from all metaphysical difficulties, I had introduced the model theory by saying that W was the set of tables, D the set of chairs and $\square$ to be understood as a universal quantifier over all tables. You would rightly have wondered what on earth this had to do with *modality*.

Consider how things work in the first-order predicate calculus. The proper names of a natural language pick out objects in the actual world (although this is to ignore notationless or fictional names). This is modelled in the semantics by val(a) being a member of the domain of a model. One-place predicates of a natural language describe things, so there corresponds to each predicate the set of things the predicate describes. This is modelled in the semantics by val(F) being a *set* of objects drawn from the domain of the model. The sentence "Joe is tall" is true iff Joe is one of the tall things. This is modelled in the semantics by Fa being true in a model iff val(a) is a member of val(F). The sentence "Joe is tall and Joe is bald" is true precisely when "Joe is tall" is true and "Joe is bald" is true. This is modelled in the semantics by the inductive clause: Fa & Ga is true in a model iff Fa is true in the model and Ga is true in the model. And so on. All this gives us is the basis of a story that (a) links the pure mathematics of the model theory to the semantics of natural language and (b) links the inductive definition of truth in a model to the intuitive notion of truth for a sentence in the language. True, there are genuine disagreements about what exactly the correct story should be, but the facts mentioned in the above paragraph at least give us the foundations on which to base an explanation of why the pure semantics can be applied to natural languages.[36]

We could tell a similar story linking the semantics of a modal natural language to possible worlds semantics. Such a story might go as follows. Names of a natural language pick out actual or possible objects (so here we might now be able to account for fictional names); this is modelled in the semantics by val(a) being a member of D. One-place predicates of a natural language describe things. Because of this, to each predicate *and* to each world, there corresponds a set: the set of things at that world that fit the description. This is modelled in the semantics by treating val(F) as a function from elements w of W to sets of $d(w)$. The sentence "Necessarily P" is true precisely when P is true at all worlds. This is modelled in the semantics by the inductive clause: $\square P$ is true in a model iff P is true at all worlds in the model. And so on.

The trouble now is that anyone who doesn't accept the existence of possible worlds, or who doesn't think that necessity is a kind of quantifier over possible worlds, could not accept this story. The pure semantics itself may not commit us to possible worlds, but the natural explanation of why possible worlds semantics has any authority in settling questions of logical truth, expressive power and the like *does* commit us to these things. This is not to say that possible worlds semantics could have no justification from one who did not believe in worlds, just that some justification must be forthcoming. Unfortunately, it has proved quite difficult to justify possible worlds semantics without accepting possible worlds.[37] Without a secure metaphysical underpinning, the results in logic are in danger of having nothing more than formal significance.

Note that both possible worlds *and* possible individuals are mentioned here in explaining why we should believe the possible worlds semantics. The picture is one where there are various worlds and various individuals existing at these worlds and having different properties at these worlds. A philosopher who provides us only with an ontology of possible worlds has not done enough to justify possible worlds semantics.

Possible worlds semantics provides one of the key links between modality and possible worlds. Few who currently work in modality reject the possible worlds framework; the two are now typically seen as a package. However, before we can even turn to the theories of possible worlds, and see whether they can be defended from various objections, we must first examine well-known objections to our very modal concepts themselves. If QML itself is conceptually incoherent then who cares about its semantics: the very theory itself must be rejected. Quine has been the biggest critic of our modal notions, and it is to his criticisms that we now turn.

3 Quinian scepticism

In the first half of the twentieth century, modality was either ignored altogether or regarded with suspicion and scepticism. Of these early modal sceptics, the most suspicious and the most sceptical was W. V. Quine. Part of Quine's scepticism stemmed from his belief that modal notions are, in some sense, not required in our philosophical and scientific theorizing.[1] As we saw in Chapter 1, this view now seems scarcely tenable. Today we see modal notions looming large in much of our everyday thought and our scientific and philosophical theorizing. Perhaps future philosophers will one day show us how the modal notions can successfully be eliminated from our theorizing, but until that work is actually done we cannot simply dismiss the modal. But Quine had other reasons for his scepticism. In Quine's view, the logical properties of modal systems are crucially different from the logical properties of his beloved first-order predicate calculus. In particular, the first-order predicate calculus is an *extensional* logic, while quantified modal logic is *intensional*. For Quine, there are grave problems in interpreting intensional logics. Quine charges quantified modal systems with giving rise to unintended sense or nonsense, committing us to an incomprehensible ontology, and entailing an implausible or unsustainable Aristotelian essentialism. In this chapter, we shall examine such Quinian arguments against the coherence of the modal. We shall see that such worries were largely misguided and that the possible worlds machinery provides us with the conceptual tools to see off all such objections.

Intensionality and compositionality

Quine is unhappy with intensional systems, and happy with extensional ones. What is the distinction? Typically, the intensional/ extensional distinction is explained by giving examples. *First-order predicate* logic is a paradigm example of an extensional logic. Different parts of this language have a certain kind of entity associated with them, and these entities are called *extensions*. The extensions of the referring terms are their *referents*: the objects that they refer to. The extensions of the predicates are the *set of things that satisfy that predicate*. Thus, for example, the extension of the predicate "*x* is red" is the set of red things.[2] Finally, the extensions of the sentence are the *truth-values* of the sentence. Now that we have said what the *extensions* are, we can say what it is for a logic to be extensio*nal*.

> *Extensionality*: Let φ and ψ be formulas or terms of our language and suppose that φ contains ψ. A language is extensional if, whenever ψ* has the same extension as ψ, and whenever φ* is the result of replacing all occurrences of ψ with ψ*, then the extension of φ is equal to the extension of φ*.

A system is *intensional* just when it fails to be extensional.

Some examples will help understand this definition. Let φ be the sentence *P* & *Q*. Let *R* have the same truth-value as *Q*. So, by the above, *R* and *Q* have the same extension. The result of substituting *R* for *Q* in φ gives us φ*, which in this case is the sentence *P* & *R*. Since the connective & is truth-functional, it is clear that *P* & *R* will have the same truth-value (and thus the same extension) as the sentence *P* & *Q*.

Consider another example. Let the predicate *Px* have the same extension as the predicate *Qx*. Let φ be the sentence $\forall x(Px \rightarrow Fx)$. It follows that, φ* is the sentence $\forall x(Qx \rightarrow Fx)$. If first-order predicate logic is extensional, then it should be the case that φ and φ* have the same extension (i.e. truth-value). We can see that they do by noting that $\forall x(Px \rightarrow Fx)$ is true precisely when the set of *P* things is a subset of the set of *F* things (recall the model theory of Chapter 2). Since, by assumption, the set of *P* things just is the set of *Q* things, the *P* things will be a subset of the *F* things precisely when the Q things are a subset of the F things. But the Q things are a sub-set of the F things precisely when $\forall x(Qx \rightarrow Fx)$. It follows that $\forall x(Qx \rightarrow Fx)$ precisely when $\forall x(Px \rightarrow Fx)$. In other words, φ and φ^* have the same truth-value and thus the same extension.

Our final example illustrates *intensionality*. Let φ be the modal sentence $\Box P$. Suppose that Q has the same truth-value (and so the same extension) as P. Then φ^* will be the sentence $\Box Q$. But here φ and φ^* can have different truth-values even if P and Q have the same truth-value. For instance, let P be the true sentence "$2 + 2 = 4$" and let Q be the true sentence "Joe is alive". Since they are both true, they both have the same extension. But $\Box P$ and $\Box Q$ have different truth-values (and so different extensions). While it is necessary that $2 + 2 = 4$ it is sadly *not* necessary that Joe is alive. So we see that, for modal systems, extensionality fails.

The first thing to note is that, if we wished, we could cut through all the supposed problems of intensionality simply by *ditching* QML and expressing all our modal theses in an extensional first-order language that quantified over possible worlds and possibilia such as PWL discussed in Chapter 2. As indicated in Chapter 2, such languages are capable of expressing everything that can be expressed in QML and more, so nothing would be lost by such a move, and it seems that worries about intensionality would be circumvented. But let us see whether we can defend QML itself from intensional worries.

It can be shown that, for first-order logic, what was true in the first two examples of extensionality above is true *in general*: one can substitute different terms or formulas with the same extension in any formula of the language without affecting its extension. In other words, the extension of the whole formula is a *function* of the extension of the parts of the formula. This sounds like a nice result, and a result that some have regarded as important. But is it?

One possible reason for thinking it important comes from the philosophy of language. If we are to explain our ability to use and understand a potentially infinite number of sentences we must suppose that the meanings of complex parts of language depend in a rule-based way on the meanings of simpler parts of language. Compositional semantics requires precisely the kind of functional dependence that we find extensional languages, such as the first-order predicate calculus, obeying. And if we also accept the popular view that the meaning of a part of language is the contribution that part makes towards determining the *truth-value* – or the *extension* – of the sentences in which it appears, it seems that a case for extensionality is emerging.

But this argument is poor. Grant the case for compositionality, and grant the view that the meaning of a linguistic item is to be understood in terms of the contribution the item makes towards determining the truth-value or extension of the complex sentences in which it appears. Still we have no argument that the truth-value of a sentence must be a function of the *extensions* of its parts, for extensions have been introduced by nothing more than *stipulation*. It was *stipulated* above that the extension of a term was its referent; it was *stipulated* that the extension of a predicate was the set of things that satisfied it; it was *stipulated* that the extension of a sentence was its truth-value. But mere *stipulations* can't do any philosophical work. The stipulations have to be justified. All that is necessary for compositional semantics is that the *meaning* of complex strings of symbols depends upon the *meanings* of its simpler parts. So far, *nothing* has been said as to why the compositional semanticist must do this using an ontology that contains only referents, extensions of predicates and truth-values.

Indeed, if it is compositional semantics for modal languages that we want, we have already seen how it can be done. The inductive definitions of ⊨ outlined in Chapter 2 are easily taken as showing us how the meaning of a complex modal sentence is a function of the meanings of the simpler words that make up the sentences. By making the usual identification of truth with truth-in-the-intended-model, where the intended model is the one where W is the set of all possible worlds, and D the set of all possible individuals, the semantic theorist has his account of how the truth-value of any complex modal sentence is a function of the meanings of the simpler sentences. The provision of a compositional semantics can be seen as yet another advantage of the possible worlds approach to modal logic.

It is true that possible worlds semantics makes use of possible worlds and possible objects. And these never appeared in the list of extensions. But the fact that we cannot use the elements in your list of extensions to give a compositional semantics for modal language and logic may not be due to a fault of the language but due to the poverty of your list. Moreover, it's not as if the idea that a theory of meaning will need entities that are not found on the list of extensions is a radical one. From the very beginning, Frege thought names had both a reference *and* a sense, and that the two were needed if we were to provide a satisfactory theory of meaning.[3] However, it is at just this point that the objection to intensional logic may become *ontological* rather than logical. If the semantic theorist requires entities other than individuals, sets and truth-values, then he had better make sure that the ontological cost of these entities is not too high, and that the entities form part of a safe and sane ontology. Yet Quine, for one, finds these entities, these "intensional"[4] objects such as those postulated by Frege and others,[5] problematic, for he thinks such entities do not have well-defined identity conditions. The trouble for Quine is that, typically, two items of language are said to have the same sense precisely when the two items have the same meaning. But, as is well known, Quine has a dim view of the notion of *synonymy* and thinks it too unstable and ill defined a notion to use in defining identity conditions.

This move still leaves us looking for a principled justification for the intensional/extensional distinction. The issue has now become one of ontology, and different philosophers have different views about which entities are safe and sane. There are plenty of metaphysicians who think that abstract objects such as sets and truth-values are no part of a plausible ontology; they're not even happy with *extensions*. Moreover, questions as to whether or not possible worlds themselves form part of a safe and sane ontology can only be answered by considering the various theories of possible worlds themselves. If other possible worlds and possible individuals are, for example, concrete objects much like the actual world and actual individuals with which we are already familiar, then there is no a priori reason to think that their identity conditions should depend upon the concept of synonymy, or indeed why they should pose any problems at all. The right theory of possible worlds, then, may very well meet Quine's objections.

To sum up, a preference for extensional languages has not been well motivated. Certainly, the principle of compositionality should be respected, and it is true that a compositional semantics cannot be given in terms of the entities we use in giving the semantics for the predicate calculus. But there is no inference from this to the thought that a compositional semantics cannot be given at all. Perhaps we do better to regard the sceptics of the intensional as offering a *challenge* rather than an argument. Perhaps they are challenging us to provide a compositional semantics. But possible worlds semanticists *can* meet this challenge; possible worlds theorists *do* have such a semantics. True, there may be ontological worries with the entities postulated by such a semantics – we may decide that the semantics is not worth the ontological cost – but the resolution of such worries comes only after the various theories of possible worlds have been examined and understood. At this stage, at least, we have no concrete reason to be sceptical of the intensional.

Referential opacity

In the previous section, we examined problems associated with a failure of extensionality in general. In this section, we examine problems that are associated with a particular kind of failure of extensionality. The particular failure at issue is that, by substituting different terms referring to the same individual in a modal sentence, the truth-value of the whole sentence is affected. Of course, by definition, extensional languages do not possess this feature. For instance, in extensional contexts, if "$a = b$" is a true identity statement, then either of the terms a and b may be substituted for each other in any true sentence S containing one of those terms, and the resulting sentence will be true. So, for instance, if the sentence "Joe is the tallest man in the class" is true, and the identity statement "Joe is the sole occupier of 7 Ormonde Terrace" is true, then we can substitute the term "the sole occupier of 7 Ormonde Terrace" for "Joe" in the first sentence and preserve its truth-value, to reach the true sentence "The sole occupier of 7 Ormonde Terrace is the tallest man in the class." In general, for any sentence of first-order quantified logic $\varphi(t)$, if $t = t^*$, $\varphi(t)$ has the same truth-value as $\varphi(t^*)$. Quine calls this feature of extensional systems *referential transparency*. Languages that lack this feature are said to be *referentially opaque*.

Modal systems are indeed referentially opaque. Here is the paradigm example. Consider the true identity statement:

(1) $9 =$ the number of planets

and the true modal sentence:

(2) Necessarily, 9 is greater than 7.

If modal contexts were referentially transparent, we could substitute the term "the number of planets" for the term "9" in sentence (2) without affecting the truth-value of (2). Performing this substitution results in the sentence:

(3) Necessarily, the number of planets is greater than 7.

But this sentence is false. Had there been five planets, it would have been true that the number of planets would have been less than 7. Therefore we cannot substitute terms that refer to the same object within modal contexts while preserving the truth-value of the relevant sentence. So modal systems are referentially opaque.

Note that, strictly speaking, the invalid argument from (1) to (3) cannot even be *expressed* in the quantified modal logic that we presented in Chapter 2. If you look again at QML, you will see that the language doesn't contain the linguistic resources capable of forming terms such as "the tallest man", "the coldest day" or "the longest night".[6] The standard way of dealing with sentences containing such definite descriptions is to paraphrase them away as Russell taught us to do. "The tallest man is tall" becomes "For any x, if x is a man taller than any other, and x is the *only* man taller than any other,[7] then x is tall." But once descriptions have been paraphrased away, it is no longer clear in what way substitutivity fails. Still, let us for the moment bracket this point and assume that a decent modal logic *ought* to have the linguistic resources to formulate descriptive referring terms, and continue exploring Quine's objection.

Some find referential opacity in and of itself a cause for concern. For instance, Wilson writes, "If identity does not mean universal interchangeability, then I do not really understand identity at all."[8] But not everyone is so bothered. Certainly, a form of argument valid for predicate logic turns out *not* to be valid in quantified modal logic. But all that follows from this is that we must rewrite the inferential rules for quantified modal logic: in particular, the principle of substitutivity must be restricted.[9] It is not at all obvious, at least to me, why referential opacity in and of itself should be a cause for concern about our modal concepts.

Quine thinks that the demand that logical systems be referentially transparent is nothing more than the formal implementation of a natural and plausible principle governing identity itself, a principle that he calls "the indiscernibility of identicals".[10] This, of course, is a humorous reference to Leibniz's principle, "the identity of indiscernibles", according to which any two things sharing all the same properties are identical. Leibniz's principle is a matter of some debate.[11] However, Quine's converse principle certainly appears plausible. Surely, if a and b are identical, if they are one and the same, then every property that a has will be had by b as well; or, in more semantic terms, anything true of a will also be true of b.[12] But while the indiscernibility of identicals is extremely plausible, it still is not immediately clear how this metaphysical principle supports the logical principle that our systems ought to be referentially transparent. Unfortunately, Quine does not help us here: he simply assumes that referential transparency just is the formal implementation of this metaphysical principle.

Linsky agrees that referential transparency lacks the self-evidence of the indiscernibility of identicals, but thinks that semantic considerations explain why the latter supports the former. In Linsky's view, "logic teaches us to analyse statements as arising from predicates by binding of their free variables or by replacement of these by singular terms".[13] For instance, logic teaches us to analyse the statement "If Socrates is a man then Socrates is mortal" as arising from the complex predicate "If x is a man, then x is mortal" by replacing the free variable that appears here with the referring term "Socrates". In general, we can think of a complex sentence φt as arising from the complex predicate φx binding the term t. Now, predicates, whether simple or complex, are simply things that are true of some objects and false of others. Accordingly, φt is true precisely when the predicate φ applies to the object denoted by t. However, if φ applies to the object denoted by t, then φ will apply to the object denoted the object denoted by t, *whatever* term we use to denote this object. In particular, if t and t^* have the same denotation, then φt will be true when φt^* is.

Although plausible, this argument is flawed. One can question whether it is even true that logic teaches us to analyse sentences in the way that Linsky says. True, in the first-order case, no harm is done by adopting Linsky's analysis. But it is a moot point whether anything in first-order logic *forces* us to regard any sentence of the form φ*t*, with φ a possibly complex predicate, as picking out an object denoted by *t*, and stating that this object falls under the extension of φ. However, even if this is granted, defenders of modal logic will claim that this argument simply begs the question: *predicate* logic may teach us to analyse sentences the way Linsky says, but what works for predicate logic may simply fail for modal logic. Indeed, a little reflection shows that Linsky's analysis is insensitive to certain scope distinctions that, in modal logic, *are* important. Consider the following two sentences:

(A) Necessarily, the tallest man is taller than any other.
(B) The tallest man is necessarily taller than any other.

It is plausible to think that (A) is true. There is nothing at all mysterious about the modality in (A): it simply follows from the meaning of the words that the tallest man is taller than any other and so this truth is necessary. But (B) is implausible. The tallest man, whoever he is, does not have the property of being the tallest man *essentially*; he might have been shorter, or the second tallest man might have grown an extra couple of inches. The modality in (A) is *de dicto*: it is the proposition "The tallest man is taller than any other" that is necessary. But the modality in (B) is *de re*: (B) should be understood as saying that the tallest man, in and of himself, is *essentially* taller than any other. Now, (B) is capable of being analysed as Linsky says. We can regard (B) as holding whenever the complex predicate "*x* is necessarily taller than any other man" applies to whatever object is denoted by the singular term "the tallest man". So, for sentences of this form, universal substitutivity should hold. But, because (A) is true and (B) is false, the sentence (A) *cannot* be correctly analysed in Linsky's terms. It would simply be wrong to think of (A)'s assertive content as equivalent to the thought that the object denoted by the singular term "the tallest man" falls under the complex predicate "*x* is necessarily the tallest man".

The *de re/de dicto* distinction shows us how to block Linsky's argument for referential transparency. Possible worlds theorists can go one better: they can show us that, in modal logic, we should *expect* referential opacity and show to exactly what degree referential opacity occurs. The argument goes as follows. Everyone should agree that there are terms that have their reference relative to a particular context. Relative to one context, the term *t* may refer to *a*; relative to another context, the very same term *t* may refer to *b*. Indexicals provide a familiar example of this. One and the same term "here" can refer to different places when uttered on different occasions. Similarly, which entities the terms "the prime minister", or "the day after tomorrow" or "last year" refer to is relative to the time. In such contexts, we do not expect referential transparency to hold. Indeed, such contexts are referentially opaque. The true sentence "At some point in the future, the prime minister will be a woman" does not entail the false sentence "At some point in the future, Tony Blair will be a woman", even though Tony Blair and the prime minister are one and the same. The reason for this failure is obvious. The phrase "At some point in the future, *P*" will be true if the proposition *P* is true at some point in the future. But, at some point in the future, "the prime minister" and "Tony Blair" will no longer refer to the same object. Accordingly, at future times, what would make "Tony Blair is a woman" and "The prime minister is a woman" true are quite different facts about the world. At future times, the embedded sentences have quite different truth-conditions. Although the two terms refer to the same object *now*, this is no guarantee that they will continue to refer to the same object. It is no wonder, then, that by substituting presently co-referring terms we can change the truth-value of sentences containing the operator "at some point in the future ...". Moreover, to analyse the sentence "At some point in the future, the prime minister will be a woman" in this way is *not* to analyse in Linsky's way: we do *not* take the sentence to be true when the object that is the prime minister satisfies the complex predicate "At some point in the future, *x* will be a woman."

The possible worlds theorist thinks that the failure of referential opacity occurs for precisely analogous reasons. Just as which object "the prime minister" refers to depends upon a context, so which object "the tallest man" refers to also depends upon a context. As things *actually* are, "the tallest man" may refer to the heaviest man, say, but in different possible situations the phrase will pick out different objects. Moreover, there are certain operators, such as "It will always be the case that ..." and "It is necessarily true that ..." that, when attached to a sentence P, ask us to consider the truth-value of P at different times or possible situations. Now, if the two terms t_1 and t_2 both refer to the same object at all possible worlds, we would expect $\Box\varphi t_1$ and $\Box\varphi t_2$ to have the same truth-value. For, referring to the same thing at all worlds, the two sentences φt_1 and φt_2 both indeed say the same thing about the same thing at each world. But where t_1 and t_2 can refer to *different* things at different worlds, this expectation fails. If there are worlds where the referents of these two expressions come apart, we have no reason at all to think that, at such a world, φt_1 and φt_2 have the same truth-value. Now, to be told that $t_1 = t_2$ is only to be told that, as things *actually* are, these terms are co-referential. But there is no implication at all from the fact that two terms actually co-refer to these terms referring to the same thing at all worlds. Even given the indiscernibility of identicals, even given that $t_1 = t_2$, we should not expect these terms to be substitutable in a complex sentence.

This is why the indiscernibility of identicals is consistent with referential opacity in modal contexts. Nothing *metaphysically* untoward is happening; the only peculiarity is *semantic*. Actually co-referring terms have different referents in different possible situations. The possible worlds treatment of necessity thus yields a satisfactory explanation of exactly why and when there is referential opacity.

Essentialism and quantifying-in

In the previous section, we noted that definite descriptions don't appear in the formal quantified modal logics that have been developed by logicians, and wondered how Quine's problems of referential opacity could arise for such systems. Quine agrees. He concedes that, if opacity is a problem worth worrying about, then it must make itself felt in the behaviour of the quantifiers and the variables. Accordingly, Quine develops an attack on modal systems that do not contain definite descriptions.

Quine distinguishes three grades of modal involvement. In Quine's view, the higher the grade of modal involvement, the less happy he is with the modal system under investigation. On the first grade, "necessity" is understood as a predicate of *sentences* – "Necessarily, 2 + 2 = 4" should really be thought of as ascribing a property to the *sentence* "2 + 2 = 4". One of the attractions of this view is that all problems of substitutivity are immediately solved. There's no inference from "Necessarily, '9 is greater than 7'" and "9 equals the number of planets" to "Necessarily, 'the number of planets is greater than 7'" because the term "9" doesn't appear referentially in the two modal sentences. Compare this with the obviously invalid inference

"9 is greater than 7" contains five words.
9 is the number of the planets.
Therefore
"The number of planets is greater than 7" contains five words.

On the second grade of modality, "necessarily" is taken to be an operator that attaches to *closed* formulas[14] or sentences. Given a sentence *P*, "Necessarily *P*" is also a sentence. At this grade of modal involvement, "Necessarily, 2 + 2 = 4" is to be understood in much the same way as we understand "It is not the case that 2 + 2 = 4" or "It is true that 2 + 2 = 4."

On the third grade of modality, "necessarily" can be used as an operator on both closed *and* open sentences. Thus we have sentences such as "Necessarily *x* is greater than 7", and the existential and universal generalizations of this sentence, such as "There is some *x* such that necessarily *x* is greater than 7." Sentences of the third grade are said to be sentences that *quantify in*, the idea being that the quantifier binds a free variable that occurs *within* the scope of a modal operator. It is this third grade of modal commitment that Quine finds absolutely intolerable. Quine thinks that quantifying-in at worst leads to nonsense and at best commits us to an untenable essentialism.

Before assessing Quine's arguments, we note that one could join Quine in rejecting the third grade of modality but be happy to accept the second grade of modality. Quine's views are normally associated with a scepticism about the modal in general, but even if one accepts only the second grade and rejects the third there is still work for a theory of modality to do. Our thought and talk of laws, supervenience and propensities, to name but three would not obviously be affected by a rejection of the third grade of modality. So, even if Quine's arguments against the third grade are successful, it would still fall a long way short of justifying his global scepticism about the modal.

What exactly does Quine think is wrong with the third grade of modality? Quine finds it hard to interpret sentences such as "∃x(necessarily, x is greater than 7)". What, he asks, is this entity that is necessarily greater than 7? The plausible answer is that it is the number 9 that is necessarily greater than 7. Yet the number 9 is nothing more than the number of the planets. But when we are asked whether it is true, of the number that numbers the planets, that it is necessarily greater than 7, we are likely to say no, for it is possible that the number of planets is less than 7. For Quine, whether or not necessity attaches to a particular object is a matter of the way in which the object is specified. If we specify the object using the name "9", we accept the truth of "∃x(necessarily, x is greater than 7)". But when we specify the object using the description "the number of planets", we think that "∃x(necessarily, x is greater than 7)" is false.

We may feel that we have seen this argument before, when studying the referential opacity of our modal language. But the fact that we have quantifiers rather than descriptions makes a crucial difference in this context. As we have seen, the referential opacity that is manifested in sentences of the form "Necessarily $(t > t^*)$" is acceptable because it can be explained by the fact that the two terms t and t^* may refer to different objects in different worlds. *But no such explanation is available in this case.* When we quantify, we abstract away from the mode of presentation or the description that we may use to individuate an object. The sentence "∃x(necessarily, x is greater than 7)" doesn't give us any kind of term with which to pick out the object x. We cannot account for the problems of "Necessarily, x is greater than 7" because we cannot even read the "necessity" as "is true at all worlds" in this context. After all, "x is greater than 7" contains a free variable. In and of itself, it doesn't even have a truth-value at the actual world. So Quine's worries about quantification into modal contexts cannot be dealt with in the same way as before.

Fortunately, Quine's argument can be met head on.[15] Quine asks us what number it is that is necessarily greater than 7, and complains that our answer changes depending upon how the number is specified. But, provided we keep a firm grip on the *de re/de dicto* distinction, we shall not fall into the confusions that Quine accuses us of. If Quine's question is interpreted as a *de re* question – which object, in and of itself, has the property of being greater than 7 necessarily – then all hands agree that if this is true of the number 9, then it is equally true of the number of the planets, for these are one and the same thing. If the proposition under consideration is *de re*, it doesn't matter how the object is specified or referred to. Quine is wrong to say that our judgements on the *de re* proposition will change depending upon how the object is specified. Of course, there is a temptation to agree with Quine when he tells us that the number of planets is not necessarily greater than 7. But this is because it is tempting to hear the proposition as a *de dicto* one – the proposition "Necessarily, the number of planets is greater than 7" is false. But this is a different proposition. The unintended sense or nonsense that Quine complains of comes not from modal contexts *per se*, but from not distinguishing the *de dicto* from the *de re* carefully enough.

What of the charge that the third grade of modal involvement commits us to some form of *essentialism*? Roughly speaking, essentialism is the view that some objects, in and of themselves, have certain properties essentially. This is rough speaking because of dispute over the notion of a property. For instance, if we accept properties such as "is either square or is not square" then essentialism becomes trivial. *Everything* has this property and has this property *essentially*. We need to be shown that quantification into modal contexts has *contentious* essentialist consequences. Unfortunately, it is totally unclear to me what these contentious essentialist consequences are supposed to be. Quine writes as if the only way in which one can avoid the unintended sense or nonsense of quantifying-in is to accept essentialism. And it may appear as though, in our response to Quine discussed above, we are forced to accept the view that, in and of itself, an object could have a property essentially. *But this is not so*. All we need to avoid Quine's argument is a distinction: the distinction between the *de dicto* and the *de re*. Quine's argument proceeded on the basis that, *if* we accepted $\exists x \Box Fx$, then different ways of thinking about the relevant F led to trouble. Our response was to say that, if one accepted $\exists x \Box Fx$, one

then stayed out of trouble by keeping a firm grip on the *de dicto*/
de re distinction. But nobody has to accept the *truth* of $\exists x \Box Fx$. If
essentialism is to be rejected, then reject this premise of Quine's
argument too. Even if we accept the *de dicto* proposition, that it is
necessary that 9 is greater than 7, it does not follow that we have to
accept that there is something such that, in and of itself, it is necessarily greater than seven. A *de re* thought does not necessarily
follow from a *de dicto* one.

Transworld identity and essentialism

Even after the development of possible worlds semantics for quantified modal logic, some philosophers worried that Quinian objections could still be maintained. In particular, there were those who
thought that Quinian worries about essentialism still lurked in the
possible worlds semantics itself. For, so these philosophers argued,
to use the machinery of possible worlds and possibilia in the semantics of modal logic, there must be a notion of *transworld identity*:
one and the same object, in and of itself, must exist at different
possible worlds. But what is it for one and the same object to exist
at different worlds? How are such objects individuated? When we
consider some possible object existing at some other possible
world, what is it about that object that makes it identical to *this*
thing at this world rather than *that* thing at this world? Certainly, if
we knew of a set of properties that *this* thing had and *only* this thing
had at all possible worlds, then these questions about transworld
identity could be settled. But the request for such a set of properties
is nothing more than the request for the *essence* of the object.

Let us try to understand exactly the sense in which possible
worlds semantics is committed to transworld identity. Suppose S is
of the form $\exists x \Diamond Fx$. If S is true in model M then S is true at w^* (the
actual world of the model) in M. For $\exists x \Diamond Fx$ to be true at the actual
world in M, there must be some object a in the domain of w^* that
satisfies $\Diamond Fx$ at w^*. For this to be so, *there must be some possible
world* w *in the model that is such that* a *satisfies* Fx *at* w. Now, the
italicized phrase is supposed to present difficulties, for the object a
was picked up at the actual world yet the italicized phrase asks us to
consider whether or not a satisfies Fx at w, where w might be a distinct world from the actual world. If a is going to satisfy Fx at w, so

the argument goes, we are going to have make sense of a's appearing in w as well as w^*. But this is nothing more than transworld identity.

Philosophers were troubled with the idea that objects exist across worlds or that there could be transworld identity. They asked how objects were to be identified across worlds. Thus Linsky asks "What does it mean to say of an object that it is identical to an object in another possible world? What is the criterion of identity across worlds?" and his conclusion is that "These questions are requests for explication of the doctrine of individual essence",[16] where an individual essence is a property that an object has necessarily, and that *only* that object could possess. However, the development of theories of possible worlds has shown that these questions are not the same. It is possible to make sense of transworld identity without having to believe in anything like essences or essential properties.

One's theory of transworld identity depends upon which theory of possible worlds one accepts. We shall see this in more detail as we look at possible worlds theories themselves. But there are plenty of theories of possible worlds where one has a notion of transworld identity without having to accept anything like a controversial Aristotelian account of essences. Here are some examples.

1. One might take possible worlds to be entities pretty much like the actual world. They, like our world, are made up of concrete individuals but, unlike our world, contain all manner of curious creatures, such as talking donkeys and walking monsters. Indeed, these other worlds literally contain actual objects as well as merely possible ones. As well as being located at this world, Joe is located at other worlds. At these other worlds he has different properties: at some, he is taller, at others he is shorter. This is how our actual Joe manages to satisfy the predicate $\Diamond Fx$ here: by literally being a part of a world w, and being F at that world. In this case, transworld identity just is identity, and one doesn't need essences to make sense of this notion.

2. Again, we might take possible worlds to be entities pretty much like the actual world. Again, like ours, they are made up of concrete individuals and contain all manner of curious creatures. However, in contrast to the situation in 1, different

worlds do not overlap: there is no entity that is part of two different worlds. But this is not to give up on transworld identity. We can preserve transworld identity by saying that Joe satisfies "*x* is short" at some other world precisely when this other world contains something that is suitably similar to Joe, a *counterpart* of Joe, and this counterpart is short. On this view, whether or not we are committed to Aristotelian essences depends upon what we think it takes for a world to contain a counterpart of Joe. If there is no common property that Joe and all his counterparts instantiate then, again, there is no commitment to any kind of contentious essentialism.

3. On quite a different view, we might think that possible worlds were more like *books* or *stories*. According to some of these stories, there are talking donkeys; according to other stories, there are unicorns and angels. And, according to one particular story, Joe is only 5'2" tall. Of course, as things actually are, Joe is 6' tall. This story misrepresents Joe, it says something false about him. But this is all that it takes for our actual Joe to satisfy "is 5'2" tall" at the story: for the story to name him and say of him that he has this height. Again, if there is no property that Joe has in each of the stories about him, there is no need to accept any kind of doctrine about essences or essential properties.

Conclusion

We have examined Quine's arguments against modal logic, and we have found them all lacking. The defenders of modal logic, be it propositional or predicate, have nothing to fear from Quine and are quite within their rights to take modal truths and modal logic seriously, and to search for a respectable theory of modality.

4 Modalism

Introduction

Modalism is the view that the correct expression and articulation of modal thought and talk should include primitive modal operators such as *necessarily* and *possibly*, but should *not* involve quantification over or reference to possible worlds or possibilia. The correct logical form of "It is possible that *P*" is simply ◊*P*. In short, modalism is the view that modal truth is not to be articulated or understood in terms of possible worlds or possibilia.

Unlike Quine, the modalist does not wish to eliminate the modal; the modalist wishes to respect our everyday thought and talk about the possible and the necessary. The modalist thinks that there is more to the world than is given by a description of what things there are, what categorical properties these things instantiate and what categorical relations these things bear to each other. But the modalist *is* sceptical about possible worlds: he does not accept worlds other than the actual one. The modalist accepts the *objectivity* of modal truth, but rejects the existence of possible *objects*. As such, the modalist wishes to avoid the unparsimonious and counter-intuitive ontology of possible worlds and possibilia while accommodating our intuitions about modal truth, two points very much in the modalist's favour. Nevertheless, by eschewing possible worlds, the modalist also eschews many of the advantages such an ontology brings. The modalist loses the unifying analyses of possibility, necessity, counterfactuals and the like that possible worlds provide. The modalist loses the elegant possible worlds semantics and the explanations for the failure of intensionality seen in

Chapter 3. The modalist loses the right to accept the results of possible worlds semantics to discover the true axioms of modal logic – or at least loses it until some reason is found for explaining why the results of possible worlds semantics can be accepted that doesn't involve the existence of possible worlds.

None of these losses is conclusive. Perhaps the overall loss in ideological economy is more than compensated for by the resulting gain in ontological economy. Or perhaps the modalist can develop alternative unifying analyses of the relevant concepts that do not rest upon the notion of possible worlds or possibilia. But even if we grant the modalist this much, it turns out that there are problems for the modalist in what should be the very heartland of the modalist position. Bracketing all considerations of the theoretical utility of possible worlds, there are certain natural modal thoughts and intuitions that cannot be articulated using simply the concepts of *possibility* and *necessity*. In this chapter we shall see that it is no easy matter to articulate certain natural and plausible theses about the structure of modality in a way acceptable to the modalist.

There could have been things that don't actually exist

At first sight, the modalist's views about the primacy of □ and ◊ seem to be closer to our normal conception of the modal than the philosopher's apparently artificial apparatus of possible worlds and possibilia. From the very beginning it may have seemed that, although we had no difficulties accepting that Joe could have been taller than Bruno, or that it is necessary that all bachelors are unmarried, or that it is contingent that grass is green, or even that Joe has his humanity essentially, it just seems wrong to treat these truths as involving other *entities*: possible worlds or possibilia. The QML sentence ◊(Rab) is just *right* about the logical form of the English sentence "Joe could have been taller than Bruno."

But as we saw in Chapter 2, there are various modal truths that resist formalization in QML, truths that can be expressed in a familiar first-order predicate logic that quantifies over possible worlds and possibilia. Numerical quantification, cross-world comparisons, supervenience claims, claims comparing the domains of various possible worlds – none of these can be formulated in a language that uses just the simple □ and ◊. Yet all these natural theses were easily and transparently expressed using the apparatus of possible worlds.

Recall from Chapter 2 one simple example of an uncontentious modal truth that cannot be formalized in QML: there could have been things that don't actually exist. Sherlock Holmes doesn't exist, but he might have. At the very least, the Holmes fiction is possible: the stories aren't true, but they could have been. In Chapter 2 we saw that $\Diamond \exists x \neg Ex$ doesn't capture the correct thought, for this says that it is possible that there is something that doesn't exist – but that there is something that doesn't exist could *not* have been true. It is clear what has gone wrong. It is not that there are worlds containing things that don't exist; rather, there are worlds containing things that don't exist *in the actual world*. Unfortunately, the modalist cannot leave it at that because this way of expressing the thought involves possible worlds.

The modalist counters that introducing possible worlds is not the only option. It is true that the sentence $\Diamond \exists x \neg Ex$ does not express the thought that there could have been things that do not actually exist, but all that follows from this is that QML is inadequate. To turn to a possible worlds language, says the modalist, would be an overreaction. What we need to do is to *enrich* QML, to give it extra linguistic resources that will allow it to express thoughts about what actually exists. After all, there is no a priori reason why we should think that QML as it stands contains all the resources the modalist needs to express his views on modality. Accordingly, there is nothing to stop the modalist from adding further modal operators to his language in order to express the modal truth.

Indeed, it is pretty clear what needs to be done with the sentence "There could have been things that don't actually exist": what is needed is some way of capturing the force of the English word "actually". Accordingly, the modalist introduces a new modal operator, **A**. **A**φ is to be interpreted as saying "actually φ". Like the operators $\Box$ and $\Diamond$, **A** has the same syntactic flexibility as $\neg$. In other words, if φ is a wff then **A**φ is a wff also. Armed with this new operator, the sentence "There could have been things that do not actually exist" can now be written $\Diamond \exists x \mathbf{A} \neg Ex$.

The possible worlds semantics of Chapter 2 can be modified in a natural way to accommodate this new operator. All that needs to be done is to add a clause for **A**. Given our intuitive grasp of the meaning of **A** it is clear how such a clause should go:

$$<W, w^*, R, D, d, \text{val}, w> \vDash \mathbf{A}\varphi \text{ iff}$$
$$<W, w^*, R, D, d, \text{val}, w^*> \vDash \varphi$$

In other words, **A**φ is true in a model iff φ is true at the actual world in the model.

There could have been more things than there actually are

Unfortunately for the modalist, even this extended modal language is not powerful enough to express all that it should. Consider the sentence "There could have been *more* things than there actually are." As a piece of pure English, this sentence uses only modal operators so we might think it could be expressible within the language developed. But this appearance is illusory.

First note that the sentence $\Diamond\exists x\mathbf{A}\neg Ex$ does not capture this thought. This can be seen by thinking in terms of possible worlds. $\Diamond\exists x\mathbf{A}\neg Ex$ says only that there are worlds containing objects that are not identical to anything that exists in the actual world. But the truth of "There could have been more things than there actually are" requires more than this; it requires the existence of worlds that, as well as containing something that doesn't actually exist, also contain every actually existing thing. Somehow we need to capture the idea that there is a possible world w such that, for any x that actually exists, x exists at that w, and w contains something that doesn't actually exist. In a possible worlds language, this presents no problem: $\exists w[\forall y(Eyw^* \rightarrow Eyw) \& \exists x(Exw \& \neg Exw^*)]$.[1] But, of course, the modalist must find another way of expressing this thought.

Perhaps the following suffices:

$$\Diamond(\forall x(\mathbf{A}Ex \rightarrow Ex) \& \exists y\neg \mathbf{A}Ey)$$

An English version of this might run "It could have been the case that everything that actually exists exists *simpliciter*, and there exists something that doesn't actually exist."

Sadly, this will not work. Consider a possible world w that contains the actual objects a, b and c, plus some new object d that is not identical to any actually existing object. Clearly, the possibility of such a world w is not enough to make "There could have been more things than there actually are" true: w doesn't contain all the actual objects. But the possibility of w *does* suffice to make $\Diamond(\forall x(AEx \to Ex) \,\&\, \exists y \neg AEy)$ true. For in w, the two conjuncts $\forall x(AEx \to Ex)$ and $\exists y \neg AEy$ are true. Clearly, in w, the second conjunct, $\exists y \neg AEy$, is true; the existence of d in w testifies to this. But, in w, $\forall x(AEx \to Ex)$ is also true. The reason for this is that, in w, the quantifier $\forall x$ ranges only over the things that exist at w. Accordingly, $\forall x(AEx \to Ex)$ is true at w if a, b, c and d all satisfy $(AEx \to Ex)$ – but since they all satisfy the consequent of this formula (for they all exist at w) they trivially satisfy the whole formula itself. Our attempted formalization fails to say what we wanted it to say.

Perhaps our error lies in insisting that the range of the quantifier $\forall x$ be restricted when it appears within the scope of a modal operator. After all, modalists are not honour-bound to accept the model-theoretic clauses given to quantified modal logic. Just because, on the model theory, the range of the quantifier is restricted to the relevant world of assessment, it doesn't follow that the modalist has to make the corresponding move in his treatment of quantified modal logic. One solution might be to treat $\forall x$ as ranging over all possible objects. But while one who believes in possibilia can treat the quantifier in this way, such an interpretation of the quantifier would be very much at odds with the parsimonious ambitions of the modalist.

However, while there are plenty of ontological qualms in accepting possibilia, there is nothing wrong with accepting actual objects, so why not rewrite the inductive definition of existential sentences to let the quantifier range over actual objects, the objects that appear in w^*, even when it appears within the scope of a $\Diamond$? Unfortunately, if we adopt the idea that the quantifier always ranges over the elements of the actual world, even when it appears within the scope of a modal operator, then it seems we can no longer allow for the truth of "There could have been things that don't actually exist." If $\exists x$ is restricted to actual objects, even within the scope of a $\Diamond$, none of the things it ranges over can satisfy $\neg AEx$.

Perhaps our problem is that we don't want the $\forall x$ to be limited by the $\Diamond$ to the things that appear in the world that we were sent to. If we could find a way of "taking the restrictions off the quantifier", if we could get it to "range over every possible object",[2] we might be able to write down a sentence with the intended sense. But wait! The modalist *can* get the effect of this in an acceptable way by using the phrase $\Box \forall x$. By saying, "Necessarily, for any x ...", or "No matter how the world is, for any x ...", we have a phrase that has the effect of ranging over all the possible individuals. The sentence "No matter how the world is and for any x, if x actually exists then x exists" will be true at a world precisely when that world contains all the things that exist at the actual world. This suggests that the problem can be solved by placing a $\Box$ before the universal quantifier as follows:

$$\Diamond \{ [\Box \forall x (AEx \to Ex)] \ \& \ \exists y \neg AEy \}$$

So does *this* sentence correctly capture our thought "There could have been more things than there actually are"? It's not easy to tell. As we have already seen, it is rarely easy to assess sentences containing nested modal operators.[3] But the modalist cannot use possible worlds semantics to help him here.

In fact, it is dubious whether this sentence says what we want it to. The trouble is with the string $[\Box \forall x (AEx \to Ex)]$. We wanted this formula to have the effect of saying "For *any* possible object, if the object exists at the actual world, then the object exists *simpliciter*." But in fact, this string just expresses the necessity of the proposition "Everything is such that, if it exists at the actual world then it exists." Adopting a possible worlds viewpoint, we can see that this is trivially satisfied. $\Box \forall x (AEx \to Ex)$ will be true at a world if $\forall x (AEx \to Ex)$ is true at all worlds w;[4] $\forall x (AEx \to Ex)$ is true at w if every object a that exists at w satisfies $(AEx \to Ex)$ at w; but since, trivially, every object that exists at w satisfies Ex at w, just by the meaning of Ex, every object a at w satisfies $(AEx \to Ex)$, since it satisfies its consequent.

We can now see what has gone wrong. The trouble is that the second (underlined) appearance of Ex in

$$\Diamond \{ [\Box \forall x (AEx \to \underline{Ex})] \ \& \ \exists y \neg AEy \}$$

falls under the scope of the $\Box$. Because of this, the second Ex fails to bring us back to the possibility introduced by the original $\Diamond$, and thus the attempt to compare the domains of two different possible worlds in this sentence fails.

We are stymied. If we leave out the $\square$ then we have

$$\lozenge[\forall x(\mathbf{A}Ex \rightarrow Ex)\ \&\ \exists y \neg \mathbf{A}Ey]$$

which fails because $\forall x$ picks up only the individuals that appear at the possible world introduced by the initial $\lozenge$. When we try to "unrestrict" the quantifier by writing

$$\lozenge\{[\square\forall x(\mathbf{A}Ex \rightarrow Ex)]\ \&\ \exists y \neg \mathbf{A}Ey\}$$

$\forall x$ now has the correct range, but the second Ex no longer refers us back to the possibility introduced by the initial $\lozenge$. We need new resources if we wish to capture the natural modal thought that the world could have contained more things than it actually does.

Before moving on to consider such new resources, we would do well to reflect on the very nature of the above discussion. Is it really clear that we are capable of assessing the *content* of such complicated sentences as

$$\lozenge\{[\square\forall x(\mathbf{A}Ex \rightarrow Ex)]\ \&\ \exists y \neg \mathbf{A}Ey\}$$

without using possible worlds to guide us? Could we see why

$$\lozenge\{[\square\forall x(\mathbf{A}Ex \rightarrow Ex)]\ \&\ \exists y \neg \mathbf{A}Ey\}$$

and

$$\lozenge\{[\forall x(\mathbf{A}Ex \rightarrow Ex)]\ \&\ \exists y \neg \mathbf{A}Ey\}$$

failed to express the thought that we wanted to express without using possible worlds semantics? After all, in the discussion above, again and again I helped myself to possible worlds talk in explaining what went wrong. I talked of: the possibilities introduced by the operators $\square$ and $\lozenge$; the domain of the quantifiers being restricted to certain worlds; and the possibilities introduced by the modal operators. The possible worlds theorist can explain what goes wrong, but how is the *modalist* to conduct the discussion? Is it so clear that, without possible worlds semantics, we would not be blind to the difference between the two and, in any case, have no idea whether or not either of them expressed the thought that the world could have contained more things than there actually are?

The modalist might counter that we have already accepted that the fundamental modal operators, □, ◊ and **A,** are reasonably well understood. And the above sentences use nothing more than these operators, plus the familiar quantificational and truth-functional devices. But it is natural to wonder whether the fact that it is so difficult to assess the content of such sentences without availing ourselves of the possible worlds machinery indicates that the modal operators are *not* as well understood as we thought. Certainly, we all understand □*P,* ◊*Q* and **A***R,* if *P, Q* and *R* are relatively simple formulas, and, in particular, if *P, Q* and *R* contain no modal operators themselves. But once the embedded formulas contain modal operators themselves, matters are not nearly as simple. There is scope for ambiguity and confusion about the way in which the modal operators and the quantifiers interact when appearing in complex sentences. Ambiguity can be resolved and confusion dispelled easily enough if we accept the possible worlds picture, but such locutions and explanations are not available to the modalist.

To summarize, the situation we have reached is that we can see that there are certain natural thoughts that cannot be formulated even in an expanded quantificational modal logic. Indeed, there is a concern that our ability to recognize which thought a modal sentence expresses involves the possible worlds picture in an essential way. It is in this sense that the possible worlds picture provides a clarification of our everyday modal concepts. In English, the sentence may not include any quantification over worlds, but when we come to assess the differences between various thoughts expressed in QML, our brute intuitions fail us and we need the possible worlds picture to clarify exactly what various sentences in the language of QML say. The discussion above shows the great power to clarify the nature of our modal discourse that possible worlds semantics delivers.

However, let us set aside our worries and return to the modalist's project to find a language capable of expressing sentences such as "There could have been more things than there actually are."

Beyond the "actually" operator

Modalists have reacted to the expressive limitations of QML by going beyond – well beyond – the "actually" operator. One way in which modalists have increased the expressive power of modal languages is by adding a denumerable number of operators to their language. For each number n, the extended language includes the operators $\Box_n$, $\Diamond_n$ and $\mathbf{A}_n$.[5] However, unlike the operator $\mathbf{A}$, which at least corresponded to our intuitive concept of "actually", it is not clear to which, if any, intuitive concept these subscripted modal operators correspond. In order for us to get some idea of how these operators work, we turn to model theory.

First, another place must be added to tuples $<W, w^*, R, D, d, \mathrm{val}, w>$; models of our new language will take the form $<W, w^*, R, D, d, \mathrm{val}, \omega, w>$, where ω is an ordered sequence of worlds. We write $\omega[v/i]$ for the result of substituting world v for the ith world in ω, and we write ω_n for the nth member of ω. Model-theoretic clauses can then be given for the new operators. They are:

$$<W, w^*, R, D, d, \mathrm{val}, \omega, v> \vDash \Diamond_n\varphi \text{ iff for some } v' \in W,$$
$$<W, w^*, R, D, d, \mathrm{val}, \omega[v'/n], v'> \vDash \varphi.$$

$$<W, w^*, R, D, d, \mathrm{val}, \omega, v> \vDash \Box_n\varphi \text{ iff for all } v' \in W,$$
$$<W, w^*, R, D, d, \mathrm{val}, \omega[v'/n], v'> \vDash \varphi.$$

$$<W, w^*, R, D, d, \mathrm{val}, \omega, v> \vDash \mathbf{A}_n\varphi \text{ iff}$$
$$<W, w^*, R, D, d, \mathrm{val}, \omega, w_n> \vDash \varphi.$$

The subscripted $\Box$ and $\Diamond$ operators interact with the subscripted A operators as follows. In evaluating a formula or subformula governed by a $\Box_n$ or $\Diamond_n$ at some world w, the operator sends us to some other world w' to evaluate the subformula governed by the operator *and* stores the world w' in the nth place of ω. If a subformula governed by a $\Box_n$ or $\Diamond_n$ contains $\mathbf{A}_n$ then we evaluate this subformula from the point of view of world w'.

With these operators the modalist is now able to capture the problematic "There could have been more things than there actually are." Recall that we ran into the following problem: either the universal quantifier fell within the scope of the first $\Diamond$ and therefore ranged only over the entities that existed at the possibility introduced by this operator; or, when we tried to ensure that the universal quantifier ranged over *all* possible entities by prefixing a $\Box$, we then found that the second *Ex* no longer referred us back to the first possibility. We want this *Ex* to be assessed from the point of view of the world that was introduced by the original $\Diamond$.

The subscripted operators enable us to do just that. The sentence "There could have been more things than there actually are" can now be formalized in the following way:

$$\Diamond_1\{[\Box\forall x(\mathbf{A}Ex \to \mathbf{A}_1Ex)] \ \& \ \exists y \neg \mathbf{A}Ey\}$$

To see why, let's go through the model-theoretic clauses.

Let's take an arbitrary model *M* and see what things have to be like in this model for the above sentence to be true. Currently, for the modal languages under question, models are of the form $<W, w^*, R, D, d, \text{val}, \omega, v>$. Let us suppose that

$$<W, w^*, R, D, d, \text{val}, <>, w^*> \vDash$$
$$\Diamond_1\{[\Box\forall x(\mathbf{A}Ex \to \mathbf{A}_1Ex)] \ \& \ \exists y \neg \mathbf{A}Ey\}$$

where $<>$ is the empty sequence.[6] By the evaluation clause for the $\Diamond_1$, this is true iff

$$<W, w^*, D, d, \text{val}, <v>, v> \vDash$$
$$\{[\Box\forall x(\mathbf{A}Ex \to \mathbf{A}_1Ex)] \ \& \ \exists y \neg \mathbf{A}Ey\}, \text{ for some world } v.[7]$$

$\Diamond_1$ behaves like a normal $\Diamond$; a sentence of the form $\Diamond\varphi$ will be true at a world *w*, precisely when φ is true at some world *v*. However, $\Diamond_1$ also tells the model to *store* the world *v* for future reference. Thus, at the sixth place of the model, this relevant world *v* appears, ready for further use.

We have a conjunction true at a model. The conjunction will be true at the model if the two conjuncts are true. This gives us:

$$<W, w^*, R, D, d, \text{val}, <v>, v> \vDash$$
$$[\Box\forall x(\mathbf{A}Ex \to \mathbf{A}_1Ex)], \text{ for some world } v$$

and

$$<W, w^*, R, D, d, \text{val}, <v>, v> \vDash \exists y \neg \mathbf{A}Ey,$$
for the same world v.

We already know how to assess this second clause. This second clause will be true at v precisely when there is some a in $d(v)$,[8] such that a is not in $d(w^*)$. In other words, v contains something that does not actually exist.

This is *part* of what we wanted to say. When trying to assert the possibility that there could have been more things than there actually are, such a possibility must at least include something that doesn't actually exist. But, as we have seen, this is not enough: the relevant possibility must also contain all the things that actually exist. If we are on the right track, then the first part of the conjunction should guarantee this. So let's see what happens when

$$<W, w^*, D, d, \text{val}, <v>, v> \vDash \Box \forall x(\mathbf{A}Ex \rightarrow \mathbf{A}_1 Ex)$$

By the clause for $\Box$ and $\forall x$, this will be true if, for any world u, and for any a in u,

$$<W, w^*, D, d, \text{val}, <v>, u> \vDash [(\mathbf{A}Ex \rightarrow \mathbf{A}_1 Ex)]<a>$$

Now, to say "for any world u and any a in u" is just like saying "for any possible object a": that is, for any object in D. So we can rewrite this more perspicuously as

For any a in D, $<W, w^*, D, d, \text{val}, <v>, u> \vDash$
$\quad (\mathbf{A}Ex \rightarrow \mathbf{A}_1 Ex)<a>$.

The main connective here is simply an "if ... then" statement. So the above will be true precisely when

For any a in D, if $<W, w^*, D, d, \text{val}, <v>, u> \vDash \mathbf{A}Ex <a>$,
$\quad$ then $<W, w^*, D, d, \text{val}, <v>, u> \vDash \mathbf{A}_1 Ex <a>$.

Now, $<W, w^*, D, d, \text{val}, <v>, v> \vDash \mathbf{A}Ex <a>$ precisely when $<W, w^*, D, d, \text{val}, <v>, w^*> \vDash Ex <a>$: that is, when a exists in w^*, the actual world. So we can rewrite the above as

For any a in D, if a is a member of $d(w^*)$ then
$$<W, w^*, D, d, \text{val}, <v>, u> \vDash \mathbf{A}_1 Ex <a>.$$

It is precisely here that the subscripted operators pay off, for, by the model-theoretic clauses for these subscripted operators, $<W, w^*, D, d, \text{val}, <v>, u> \vDash \mathbf{A}_1 Ex <a>$ precisely when $<W, w^*, D, d, \text{val}, <v>, v> \vDash Ex <a>$. Because of the way in which this subscripted "actually" operator works, the formula forces us to assess the existence claim from the point of view of the world v, introduced by the original $\Diamond_1$. And $<W, w^*, D, d, \text{val}, <v>, v> \vDash Ex <a>$ will be the case precisely when a exists at v.

Putting all this together gives us that the original sentence $\Diamond_1\{[\Box \forall x(\mathbf{A}Ex \rightarrow \mathbf{A}_1 Ex)] \ \& \ \exists y \neg \mathbf{A}Ey\}$ will be true in a model precisely when there is a world v such that every possible object that exists at the actual world also exists at v and v contains something that doesn't actually exist. This is exactly what we wanted. Success: our original sentence says exactly what we want it to say.

We have now seen how these new operators work and we have seen how the modalist can capture the thought that there could have been more things than there actually are. But what are we to make of these new modal operators? Are they really free of any commitment to the possible worlds picture? Are they really conducive to modalism?

Competing theories or notational variants?

In this section I shall argue that the structural and grammatical similarities between a modal language that includes subscripted modal operators and a first-order language that quantifies over worlds is enough to make us worry that such subscripted operators are not really an alternative to possible worlds talk: they are merely a *notational* variant on such talk and, as such, are metaphysically impotent.

If we find ourselves saying certain things whose truth commits us to a particular kind of entity, then we do not get rid of that commitment simply by changing notation. The sentence "Snow is white" as much entails the existence of snow as the sentence "La neige est blanche." Simply changing the words with which we express a particular thought does nothing to get rid of unwanted ontological commitment. However, it is not at all clear that the language the modalist has now developed *is* anything other than a notational variant on a language that contains quantification and variables for worlds. Those who believe in possible worlds can write sentences such as "There could have been more things than there actually are" as

$$\exists w_1[\forall w \forall x (Exw^* \to Exw_1) \,\&\, \exists y(\neg Eyw^*)]$$

Modalists will formulate this thought using sentences such as

$$\Diamond_1\{[\Box \forall x (AEx \to A_1Ex)] \,\&\, \exists y \neg AEy\}$$

The structural similarities between the two sentences is striking:

$$\exists w_1(\forall w \forall x (Exw^* \to Exw_1) \,\&\, \exists y(\neg Eyw^*))$$

$$\Diamond_1\{[\Box \forall x (AEx \to A_1Ex)] \,\&\, \exists y \neg AEy\}$$

Where once we had the clearly quantificational $\exists$ and the variable w_1, now we have the operator $\Diamond_1$. Where once we had the symbol Exw_1, now we have Ex preceded by the operator A_1. Where once we had the symbol Exw^*, now we have the symbol AEx.

Were I a linguist who came across an unknown tribe who used the subscripted boxes and diamonds in this way, and were I to notice such close grammatical and structural similarities between the sentences that this tribe wrote and the sentences of a first-order language that quantified over worlds, I would be strongly tempted to conclude that what we had was not a totally new way of thinking about modality, but merely just a slightly different notation for making the same old claims about modal reality.

This is not how things usually are when we are engaged in the project of ontological reduction by paraphrase. In most cases of ontological reduction by paraphrase, the paraphrase has a different syntactic structure from those sentences they are paraphrasing, and it is this difference of structure that gives us reason to think that we have eliminated the unwanted ontological commitment. The paraphrases are supposed to give us the true logical form of the proposition and thus show us the correct form of the fact that makes the sentence true. Let's just look at some standard examples:

1. *Numerical quantification*. When we find that "Three is the number of heads of Fido" can be paraphrased as

   $\exists x \exists y \exists z (x$ is a head of Fido & y is a head of Fido & z is a head of Fido & $\neg x = y$ & $\neg x = z$ & $\neg y = z)$

   we see that the fact that makes the sentence true does not consist in there being some object identical to the number of heads of Fido, but consists in there being something, something else and something else again that all satisfy a particular property. In the paraphrase, no abstract object is either mentioned or quantified over. And since we can see that there is a procedure for eliminating all numerical quantification in favour of this iterated quantificational procedure, we can see that this kind of numerical quantification can be paraphrased away.

2. *Average men*. "The average man has 2.4 children." On the face of it, this sentence appears to have a subject–predicate form. It appears to be saying, of this strange object the average man, that it has this strange property of having 2.4 children. Such madness cannot be tolerated! Paraphrase reveals a quite different structure to the sentence: "The number of children divided by the number of men equals 2.4." Put that way we find no quantification or reference to any peculiar things such as average men, and nothing has the property of having 2.4 children.

Unlike these cases, the structure of the sentences that the modalist now produces is strikingly similar to the structure of the sentences that those who quantify over possible worlds use in order to express their modal views. So similar are they that some might be moved to say that they no longer regard the resulting language as giving a *paraphrase* of the original language at all; it has now become nothing more than a notational variant of the original language.

A modalist might respond that we do well to attend to the structural *differences* between the modal language and a first-order language that quantifies over possible worlds as well as the similarities, for there are certain things that those who quantify over worlds can say that simply have *no* counterpart in the modalist language. For instance, those who quantify over worlds can formulate sentences such as $\forall w(w = w)$, which has no real counterpart in the modalist language. After all, if subscripted "actually" operators really were world variables, if subscripted $\Box$s really were quantifiers over worlds, then this statement would correspond to $\Box_1(\mathbf{A}_1 = \mathbf{A}_1)$. But this is not even a wff in the modalist's language. Now, identity statements are traditionally bound up with questions of objecthood. "No entity without identity" is one of Quine's well-known slogans: no object should be admitted into our ontology unless its identity conditions, the conditions that say *which* object it is, have been settled. So the fact that such identity statements are not even wffs may be taken to support the view that the modalist, in employing his subscripted modal operators, is not committed to possible worlds after all.

It is not clear to me exactly what can be read into the fact that identity statements are inexpressible in the modalist language. After all, we do not avoid ontological commitment simply by *refusing* to assert identity statements. "No entity without identity" is a normative maxim: we should only allow a kind of entity into our ontology if we can adequately fix its identity conditions. But this condition is independent of whether, as a matter of fact, we do say that a certain type of entity exists. After all, the first-order predicate calculus *without* identity is a perfectly reasonable logical language. Yet the fact that it is incapable of expressing identity conditions does not imply that the symbols $\forall$ and $\exists$ are not quantifiers, or that the sentence $\exists xFx$ does not imply a commitment to there being such things as *F*s. No. Following Quine again, when we are wondering whether or not a theory is committed to a certain kind of entity, look not to the identity statements contained within the theory, but to the quantifiers. And, in so far as the structural similarities between the modal language and first-order languages that quantify over worlds suggest that the new subscripted modal operators *are* nothing more than notional variants of the familiar quantifiers, it is difficult to believe that the modal language that has been developed is really free of commitment to possible worlds.

Modalists have defended their view from the charge that the modal operators are nothing more than quantifiers over worlds by claiming that the subscripts actually function as scope indicators:[9]

they serve to distinguish syntactic from semantic scope. Consider, for example, the formula $\Diamond_1\varphi\Diamond_2 A_1\psi$. Although syntactically the ψ falls under the scope of the second $\Diamond$, the subscripted operators show that, semantically, it is attached to the first $\Diamond$. However, making sense of this idea is not entirely straightforward. I know what it is to consider a particular proposition. And I know what it is to consider whether that proposition is *possible* or whether it is *necessary*, or whether it is *actual*. I know what it is to consider a particular object. And I know what it is to consider whether or not that object has a certain property *essentially* or merely *contingently*. But, to me at least, that is as fine grained as my intuitive understanding of these modal operators goes. When wondering about the modal status of a particular proposition, I have no sense of there being many different possible "scopes" that this modal status might affect.

Certainly, there are ways in which we could understand the subscripted modal operators as marking scope distinctions. Interpret $\Diamond_n\varphi$ as saying "There is some world n such that, at n, φ is true" and interpret A_n as "at world n". In English, whenever we meet the phrase "at world n", whatever clause follows it is interpreted as about world n. In other words, any sentence of the form "At world n, φ is the case" is true iff φ is the case at world n. Such phrases can make distinctions between semantic and syntactic scope, yet they cannot be legitimately used by a modalist, since these phrases clearly make a demonstrative reference to worlds.

As well as worrying about the structural similarities between the two languages, we can also question whether we can even grasp the subscripted modal operators without appealing to the possible worlds formalism. We already found interpreting sentences of the modalist's language difficult, even before the subscripted operators were introduced. But can the subscripted operators be understood at all without assuming some kind of possible worlds picture? At least when the simple "actually" operator, A, was introduced to us, we had a grasp of the meaning of this operator independent of the possible worlds picture. We can accept that $A\varphi$ is true precisely when φ is true in the actual world without having to accept any possible worlds into our ontology other than the actual one. We might even admit that the model-theoretic clauses for this operator do indeed assign truth-values to sentences containing the term that are faithful to our intuitive, and possibilia-free, understanding of the word "actually". However, we have no such independent grasp of the meaning of the subscripted diamonds and "actually" operators. They were introduced solely through the evaluation clauses in the model theory, and our understanding of them is gained entirely via their model-theoretic clauses. These model-theoretic clauses use the apparatus of possible worlds. To assess the truth of $\Diamond_1\varphi$ we must go to some world w, store it, and see if φ is true there; to understand $\mathbf{A}_1\varphi$ we go to the world stored by the preceding $\Diamond_1$, and see whether φ is true there. But if this is our grasp on the subscripted operators then I cannot see how we can ever meaningfully or truthfully use these operators while denying that there exists a plurality of possible worlds.

Modalists cannot use possible worlds semantics to give the meaning of the modal operators, for they do not think that possible worlds semantics paints a faithful or accurate picture of modal reality. What the modalist has to do is find some fragment of English, free from a commitment to possible worlds, or some possible worlds-free notion with which he can explain the meaning of these new operators. But modalists rarely do this. For instance, when Peacocke introduces these operators he writes:

> However many modal operators separate an indexed operator "$\Box_i$" (say) from its associated "$\mathbf{A}_i$" (or string of them), in evaluating the clause governed by the associated "$\mathbf{A}_i$" we turn our attention to the world originally being considered in evaluating the clause by the original "$\Box_i$".[10]

Such an explanation is not available to a genuine modalist. The question of whether the modalist can understand his own primitives remains.

Conclusion

The modalist faces serious difficulties and obstacles finding a possible worlds-free language capable of expressing certain relatively simple modal truths. Interpreting and understanding the sentences of his extended modal language proved to be no easy issue and, again and again, we found ourselves resorting to the language and framework of possible worlds. So far we have only examined one kind of modal truth which QML cannot express. In order to deal with others, the modalist's favoured language is going to become even more complex: even more difficult to interpret. For instance, the extensions of QML that have been examined so far cannot deal with modalized comparatives such as "My car could have been the same colour as yours actually is." The reason is that, in this sentence, the word "actually" does not appear to be functioning as an operator, acting on wffs to form other wffs. Neither $\Diamond \mathbf{A}(Rab)$ nor $\mathbf{A}\Diamond(Rab)$ (where Rxy means "x is the same colour as y", a refers to my car and b refers to your car) succeeds. Speaking intuitively, we want to put the $\mathbf{A}$ operator *inside* the predicate, and write something like $\Diamond(Ra\mathbf{A}b)$, but we await a proper, logical introduction to a concept capable of behaving in this way.

What may make us particularly pessimistic about the prospects for modalism is that problems have arisen even for sentences that, intuitively, should be relatively straightforward for the modalist to deal with. So far we have only been considering modal sentences that, at least at the level of surface grammar, seem not to involve any reference or quantification over possible worlds or possibilia. We have not even begun to consider truths such as "There are many different ways the world could have been", "There are three ways Joe could win his chess match", "Given the laws of nature, there are just two possible ways in which the system could evolve" and the like. In such cases of numerical quantification, it is obscure how the modalist is to proceed. The modalist has his work cut out for him finding a language that is capable of expressing all that he needs.

Extreme realism

Realism about possible worlds: methodological preliminaries
We now turn our attention to those metaphysicians who take the picture of possible worlds seriously and who think that possible worlds model theory *does*, in some sense, correspond to the modal facts about the world and that possible worlds should be used in the analysis of our everyday modal claims.

How can we assess different realisms about possible worlds? What criteria should guide us in our theory choice? There are two main presuppositions that underpin the possible worlds debate. These presuppositions should not be seen as unique to the debate in modality. Rather, they have lain behind the resurgence of metaphysics that has been seen in philosophy over the past 50 years.

With some exceptions, most of our pre-theoretic modal beliefs do *not* have a quantificational form. Although the modalist found certain modal sentences, such as "There could have been more things than there actually are" and modalized comparatives problematic, expressing these thoughts in English does not require explicit quantification or reference to possible worlds. Moreover, even if we accept that model theory does truly represent the kinds of states of affairs that make modal sentences true, or that modal sentences are to be formulated by quantification and reference to possible worlds, we say almost *nothing* about the nature of these worlds. Accepting the biconditional "$\Diamond P$ iff there is a possible world w such that, at w, P" commits us to an ontology of possible worlds (provided, of course, we accept there are some truths of the form $\Diamond P$), but tells us very little about what these worlds are like. True, we know that, since it is possible that donkeys talk, then accepting the biconditional implies that there must be a world such that, at w, donkeys talk. But the nature of such a world, and the nature of the operator "at w" are very much left open. Possible worlds might be maximal spatiotemporal sums, like the actual world, and "A donkey talks at w" may be true in virtue of w containing as a part a real talking donkey. But, for all that the biconditional says, possible worlds might also be particularly complex books, and "A donkey talks at w" may be true in virtue of the sentence "There is a talking donkey" appearing within the book w.

If the mere acceptance of this biconditional does not determine the nature of possible worlds, then how *are* we to determine their nature? After all, whatever their nature, our access to possible worlds is not like our access to tables and chairs. Possible worlds can't be examined, taken apart or kicked around. A merely possible world is not the kind of thing that can be observed. So what considerations can we appeal to?

In the 1930s and 1940s, when a rather brutal form of logical positivism held sway, and it was thought that the only way we could know the existence or the properties of any kind of entity was by verifying it through the senses, questions about the nature of possible worlds would have been regarded as meaningless. But when this kind of strong verificationism is pushed to its logical conclusion, it turns out that just about everything, save for a few propositions about our immediate sense experience, becomes meaningless. Although the intentions of the verificationists may have been to curb the worst excesses of metaphysics, a strict verificationism rules out far too much for comfort. Much of the positivists' beloved science, particularly the theoretical parts, fails their principle of meaningfulness. After all, if statements about the external world cannot be strongly verified (for Descartes's scheming, dream-inducing demon is, at the very least, a possibility and compatible with what we sense), if statements about the past cannot be strongly verified (for it is at least compatible with what we see that the whole universe was created 15 minutes ago), if statements about electrons and quarks and space-time cannot be strongly verified (for it is at least compatible with the evidence that our scientific theories are radically mistaken about what microscopic and unobservable entities there are), then strict verificationism leaves us with very little that is meaningful.

Once one weakens verificationism, and allows other criteria to help decide the best overall theory, the picture is quite different. Many philosophers now concede that it is rational to accept a proposition not because we can directly verify it but because it is supported by considerations of simplicity (of which ontological and ideological parsimony are important ingredients), theoretical utility, explanatory power and/or intuitive plausibility. Certainly, it is consistent with what we directly observe that the universe could have been created 15 minutes ago, with all our memories in a particular state. There's no direct *observation* we could make that could refute it. But this does not mean that the hypothesis is nonsense or that it cannot be rationally rejected. To suppose that the universe came into existence 15 minutes ago in such an amazing state that, when we look at the sky, the light travelling through space has been arranged as if to come from stars that existed millions of years ago, and that your brain and my brain came into a state that, by pure coincidence, share memories of apparently past events that actually never happened, is implausible and unlikely. Contrast this with the natural picture of things having existed for millions of years when, instead of postulating infinitely many brute coincidences, we have a natural explanation for the fact that the light coming from the skies is arranged the way it is, and a natural explanation for the fact that you and I and others remember the same things happening.

As well as using such principles of simplicity, explanatory power and theoretical utility in determining the best theory, we must also use our pre-theoretic beliefs about what is possible and necessary to guide us. For instance, the identification of possible worlds with actual concrete books keeps our ontology simple; nothing over and above actual concrete objects is postulated. However, this identification fails to respect the truth of the biconditional "$\lozenge P$ iff there is a world at which P is true". After all, for every n, it is possible that there be exactly n things. Accordingly, the biconditional yields infinitely many different possible worlds. But there are only finitely many concrete books. So possible worlds cannot be identified with concrete books after all.

Even here, we should note that no pre-theoretic belief about modality is absolutely sacrosanct. Perhaps a particularly attractive theory of possible worlds, one that is ontologically and ideologically parsimonious and that makes room for most of our pre-theoretic modal beliefs, is unable to generate worlds at which there are more objects than there actually are. Under such circumstances, one might urge that our pre-theoretic beliefs are in error and that, when the overall picture is taken into consideration, the wisest course of action is to give up the belief that there could have been more objects than there actually are.

Different theories of possible worlds must be weighed and judged on a cost–benefit basis: the lower the costs and the greater the benefits, the better the theory. The more concepts it takes as primitive, the greater the ontology it postulates and the greater the rift between the theory and common sense, then the greater are its costs; the wider the range of notions the theory can analyse and unify, the greater the number of problems the theory is capable of solving, and the greater the number of our intuitive judgements about modality the theory can preserve, the greater its benefits. Accordingly, to compare different theories, we should examine their explanatory scope and take care to note their ontological and ideological primitives.[1]

The metaphysics of extreme realism

We now turn to an extreme realism about possible worlds: the view that there are infinitely many other possible worlds and that these possible worlds are, in many respects, pretty much like the actual one. Some of these other worlds contain creatures that are literally made of flesh and blood, others contain spirits and ghosts and yet others contain things that look and behave very much like you and I do.

There's no denying that, at first sight, this hypothesis seems shocking and outrageous; it is too wild, too fantastical, too *extreme* to merit serious attention. But, thanks to David Lewis, who has forged this idea into the most comprehensive, comprehensible and detailed theory of possible worlds, one can now see that extreme realism offers the greatest benefits of all possible worlds theories currently on offer. Indeed, arguably, it is the one theory that truly delivers on all counts. In this chapter, I shall examine some well-known objections to Lewis's theory, and argue that they are indecisive. Without a knock-down argument, the decision to choose or reject extreme realism must be made by weighing and judging the advantages and disadvantages.

It's natural to say that the extreme realist's worlds are *concrete* entities. This is close to the truth, but should be handled with some care. First, we might think that there are some worlds that contain *only* abstract entities. Possible worlds, like the actual world, are nothing more than the mereological sum of the possibilia that exist there, and since a mereological sum of abstract entities is itself an abstract entity, the extreme realist's worlds may well be abstract (although, as we shall later see, in Lewis's articulation of extreme realism this possibility is actually ruled out). Secondly, the abstract/ concrete distinction itself is a matter of some debate. Perhaps it is better, then, to characterize the extreme realist as holding that a possible world represents that so-and-so is the case by so-and-so *really being the case there* (although this will have to be qualified slightly to allow for the theory of counterparts). For instance, a possible world represents that a donkey talks by it really being the case that a donkey talks there. On this theory, there is nothing particularly special about the actual world (other than the fact that we happen to be a part of it) that distinguishes it from any of the other possible worlds. Just as the actual world is the mereological sum of the objects that it represents as existing, so are possible worlds mereological sums of the objects that they represent as existing. Just as the actual world contains causally efficacious objects, so do other possible worlds contain causally efficacious objects. Just as the actual world contains objects extended in space and time, so do other worlds contain objects extended in space and time. Just as this world contains a donkey, so there are worlds containing duplicates of that donkey, things that share all the qualitative[2] intrinsic properties of the actual donkey. Indeed, there may be possible worlds that are duplicates of the actual world.

Extreme realism implies that there are things that do not actually exist. In other words, that there are non-actual objects. One might have thought that this was not a distinctive feature of extreme realism: that *any* kind of realism about possible worlds would entail the existence of non-actual objects. But this plausible line of thought is in fact mistaken. Consider the view that possible worlds are nothing more than books. According to some of these books there are talking donkeys, and according to others there are walking centaurs. What these books say is not true, but the books themselves are parts of the actual world, and thus the books themselves do indeed actually exist. It truly is a distinctive feature of extreme realism that there are things that do not actually exist.

"There are some things that do not actually exist" is, of course, counter-intuitive. But some philosophers have complained that it is worse than counter-intuitive, it is unintelligible, akin to asserting the paradoxical "There are things that do not exist."[3] This objection is mistaken. For the extreme realist, to say "There are some things that do not actually exist" is just to say that there are things that are not part of the actual world. Since, for the extreme realist, the actual world is not everything, there is no sense in which he is committed to things that don't exist *simpliciter*. "There are some things that do not actually exist" is as unproblematic as the sentence "There are some things that do not exist in London."

Although the hypothesis that there are things that do not actually exist is a counter-intuitive one, possible worlds and possible objects are not themselves strange objects. Indeed, we are to think of them as analogous to the actual world and actual objects: nothing more than mereological sums of their parts. But although on this view possible worlds are nothing more than mereological sums of possible objects, not *any* mereological sum of possible objects counts as a possible world. For instance, both you and I are possible objects, but our mereological sum is not a possible world. What distinguishes those mereological sums that are possible worlds from the mereological sums that are not?

Lewis has suggested the following way of individuating worlds. He notes that, although possible worlds themselves may be spatio-temporally extended, neither possible worlds nor objects that exist in different possible worlds are spatiotemporally related to one another. Thus, if *a* and *b* are in different worlds, *a* and *b* are not spatiotemporally related. The converse, that if *a* and *b* are not spatiotemporally related, then *a* and *b* are in different worlds, is much more contentious. Nevertheless, something like these two principles are the principles Lewis accepts for saying precisely when two objects are part of the same world. Possible worlds can then be defined as the biggest mereological sum of objects that are spatio-temporally related. In other words, possible worlds are precisely the maximal sums of spatiotemporally interrelated objects. For this definition to go through, the ideological machinery of extreme realism must be able to express "x is a part of y" and "x is spatio-temporally related to y".

The predicate "x is a part of y" should be acceptable to everyone. Independently of modality, we have excellent reason to use this predicate to state facts about composite objects. The acceptance of extreme modal realism, then, does not result in a loss of ideological parsimony in this regard. Similarly, we might think that the predicate "x and y are spatiotemporally related" should be acceptable to everyone – after all, everyone agrees that there are things that stand in such relations. Again, we might think that an extreme realist is free to use such a predicate. However, it's not clear that life is quite so simple for the extreme realist. After all, the particular spatiotemporal relation that is acceptable to all is the one that is actually instantiated by things in the concrete world – a world that we currently think obeys general relativity. Perhaps, in other worlds, different kinds of spatiotemporal relations are instantiated. Perhaps the relation that different points of space-time bear to each other in a Newtonian world is not the same as that which different points of space-time bear to each other in a relativistic world. But the extreme realist needs a principle for individuating different *possible* worlds. There are questions, then, as to whether the necessary concept of spatiotemporal relatedness is freely available to an extreme realist, or whether he must accept a new primitive predicate in this theory: a manoeuvre that costs in terms of the ideological economy to the theory.

Transworld identity

One and the same object – Joe, say – could have been six feet tall and could have been five feet tall. In possible worlds terms, this becomes the claim that there is an individual x, and there are worlds w_1 and w_2 such that x is six feet tall at w_1 and x is five feet tall at w_2. But if x itself has these two different properties at these two different worlds then x itself must exist at these two worlds. A question of transworld identity then arises: from a metaphysical point of view, what is it for one and the same thing to exist at different possible worlds?[4]

At first sight, it doesn't seem as if there should be much room for discussion here. If transworld identity is the issue, then one and the same thing must exist at the two different worlds; after all, that's what "identity" *means*. So it *seems* to follow that different worlds will contain one and the same object. But now Lewis's theory is in trouble. A possible world was supposed to be a maximal spatio-temporally related sum of possible objects, but if Joe occurs in different possible worlds then such a sum will include the things spatiotemporally related to Joe in the world where he is five feet tall, *plus* the things spatiotemporally related to Joe in the world where he is six feet tall.

This line of thought is mistaken: transworld identity does not entail the existence of objects that are part of more than one world. For comparison, notice that there are serious issues in the philosophy of time over what constitutes trans-*temporal* identity. Yes, we have a notion of one thing existing at t_1, and the same thing existing at t_2, but it doesn't immediately follow from this that there must be one and the same thing wholly present at the two moments. We might be four-dimensional objects, literally spread out in time as we are in space, and Joe at t_1 is the same as Joe at t_2 if these are three-dimensional slices of some causally continuous four-dimensional worm. The point is this: all that the possible worlds talk requires is that sense be made of the notion of one object *existing at* different worlds. Since different theorists have different views about what it is for a particular object to *exist at* a world, there is room for different accounts of transworld identity.

Lewis denies that an object a need be a part of two different worlds for that object to be five feet tall at one and six feet tall at another. Rather, all that needs to be the case for it to be true that a is five feet tall at w, is for w to contain some object b that is *relevantly similar* to a, and for that object to be five feet tall. b is called a "counterpart" of a. In general, statements of the form $\Diamond Fa$ are true iff there is some world w containing a counterpart a, such that the counterpart is F.

The counterpart relation is to be understood as a relation of similarity. As Lewis admits, the notion of similarity is vague and context dependent, but Lewis does not believe that this is a problem since he holds that, to a certain degree, *de re* modal statements *are* vague and context dependent. In one context, it might be right to think of people as having their humanity essentially. In another, we might allow the possibility that we could all have been machines. In a strange way, Lewis's views about the vagaries of *de re* modal statements have a Quinian flavour; in different contexts our views about the truth-values of one and the same modal sentence may be different. However, unlike Quine, Lewis wishes not to eliminate modal thought and talk because of such vagaries, but merely to give an account of them. Moreover, it would be an overreaction to think that, because such thought and talk does suffer from such vagaries, we should regard such thought and talk as contentless. Once the context is fixed, once the vagueness is made precise, our modal statements can still have a determinate content.

The counterpart relation is a relation of similarity, but note that similarity is quite different from resemblance. Two objects resemble each other only if they share certain *intrinsic* properties, but the extrinsic properties that the objects instantiate may play a part in making those two objects similar: similar objects may not always share their intrinsic properties. For instance, what objects count as an individual's parents may be more important in determining that individual's counterpart at a world than the intrinsic properties of the individual.

It is natural to criticize Lewis's theory of counterparts along the following lines:

> if we say "Humphrey might have won the election (if only he had done such and such)" we are not talking about something that might have happened to *Humphrey* but to someone else, a "counterpart". Probably, however, Humphrey could not care less whether someone *else*, no matter how much resembling him, would have been victorious in another possible world.[5]

But the first statement is just false. If we say "Humphrey might have won the election" we *are* talking about something that might have happened to Humphrey, and we are not talking about what *might* have happened to someone else. Rather, it is in virtue of the fact that someone who resembled Humphrey *has* (not *might have had*) the property of winning, that our very own Humphrey *might* have won.[6]

Perhaps the crucial point is really that Humphrey is *interested* or *concerned* or *cares* only with what might happen to him, and is not concerned with what *does* happen to someone who resembles him in certain respects. But if such arguments cut any philosophical ice, then just about every substantive philosophical theory would be refuted by considerations such as these. Such considerations would refute Frege's set-theoretic version of the *ancestor* relation, for Humphrey is interested in (concerned, cares) whether or not Bumphrey is his ancestor, and not with whether Bumphrey is a member of some complicated set. They would refute Tarski's set-theoretic version of *logical consequence*, for Humphrey is interested in (concerned, cares) whether or not φ is a logical consequence of ψ, and not whether any set-theoretic model in which ψ is true also makes φ true. They would refute Turing's analysis of computability, for Humphrey is interested in (concerned, cares) whether or not f is *computable*, and not whether there is a Turing machine that computes it. Such considerations of interest and concern would also refute the view that possible worlds are *abstract* entities, since Humphrey is presumably not interested in whether or not there is an abstract entity according to which he wins.

Another line of attack against Lewis's theory of transworld identity comes from Plantinga.[7] According to Plantinga, one property that Joe exemplifies necessarily is the property of being identical to Joe. But since Joe is numerically different from all his counterparts, not one of them exemplifies the property of being identical to Joe.

In possible worlds terms, there are two truths that we could take "Joe necessarily has the property of being identical to himself" to express. First, we may take it to mean that, at all worlds where Joe exists, he is identical to himself. On Lewis's theory, this will be analysed as "each counterpart of Joe is identical to itself": a sentence that is trivially true. Secondly, we might take the sentence to mean that, at all worlds where Joe exists, he is identical to our *actual* Joe. On this reading, the sentence turns into a thesis about transworld identity, relating, as it does, merely possible Joes to the actual one. But, as with identity through time, identity across worlds may not be the same as numerical identity. On Lewis's view, it is the counterpart relation that plays the role of identity across worlds, and what it is for an other-worldly Joe to be identical to the actual Joe is for these two things to be *counterparts*. Accordingly, the second reading for Lewis amounts to this: "all counterparts of Joe are counterparts of Joe" – again, a trivial truth.

Modal paradise

How does extreme realism do on the cost–benefit analysis? As far as the benefits are concerned, Lewis's theory has considerable advantages.

First, there is no trouble in getting a semantics for modal thought and talk, for the extreme realist can use his possible worlds and possibilia to express modal thought and talk in a first-order language capable of quantifying and referring to other worlds and possible objects.[8] The semantics for such a language will then be nothing more than the familiar model-theoretic semantics for first-order languages.

Secondly, the extreme realist has no difficulty in accommodating the kinds of modal truths that we found were not expressible in quantified modal logic. His acceptance of possible worlds and possible individuals allows him to analyse all these kinds of thoughts in a straightforward way. Numerical quantification, such as "There are three ways in which Joe could win the chess match", is treated as genuine quantification over sets of worlds.[9] "There could have been more things than there actually are" is treated as "There is a world w that contains a counterpart of every actually existing thing and, moreover, w contains an object that is not the counterpart of any actually existing thing." Finally, modalized comparatives, such as "My car could have been the same colour as your car actually is" can be written as "There is a world w containing a counterpart c of my car, and c is the same colour as your actual car."[10]

This treatment of the modalized comparative illustrates a benefit of Lewis's treatment of transworld identity. The phrase "c is the same colour as your actual car" expresses nothing more than that the familiar two-place *same-colour* relation holds between one object, your actual car, and an object in some other world, c. If it were the case that my car and your car were literally parts of different worlds, such a treatment simply would not work. Under such conditions, the *same-colour* relation wouldn't hold *simpliciter* between different objects; rather, we would have to say something like "My car at w is the same colour as your car at w^*."[11] It's not entirely clear how to analyse this statement. It's wrong to take it as expressing that the familiar two-place relation *same-colour* holds between my car at w and your car at w^*: what exactly is this special entity my-car-at-w supposed to be? We could, perhaps, add extra places to the predicate, so that *same-colour* turns out to be a *four*-place relation, but now we might complain at the extra ideological economy that turns out to be needed to express the modalized comparative: as well as our familiar predicate "*x* is the same colour as *y*", we now need a new predicate "*x* at *w* is the same colour as *y* at *v*." Besides, we might complain, *same-colour* just is a two-place relation. Hasn't something gone terribly wrong with our metaphysics if we find ourselves having to treat it as a four-place relation? Lewis's counterpart theory might at first sight seem counter-intuitive but, as we can see, it has its advantages.

The possible worlds analysis of counterfactual conditionals and the like goes through without any difficulties. Moreover, extreme realism also promises a very special advantage, an advantage few other theories of modality promise. The extreme realist promises to provide a *reductive* analysis of the concepts *necessarily* and *possibly*, for, in his account of what possible worlds are, the extreme realist did not use any primitive modal notions. We shall see that most theories of possible worlds do not share this advantage; most of the other theories must use the concept of possibility in defining what a possible world is.[12]

Such benefits come with little cost to the ideological economy of the theory. As we have seen, the definition of possible worlds may require the extreme realist to accept a new primitive predicate to get the effect of otherworldly spatiotemporal relations, but this is the only way in which there is even a threat to the overall ideological economy of the theory. For instance, in the possible worlds analysis of counterfactuals, the counterfactual "If *A* were the case then *B* would be the case" is true when *B* is true at the *closest* world where *A* is true. This notion of *closest* is to be understood in terms of a familiar relation: *similarity*. As we already saw when discussing counterpart theory, *similarity* is a familiar notion, and since most philosophers accept that different things are similar *irrespective* of their views about modality, we have independent reasons for using such a predicate in our theory. Because of this, the extreme realist's analysis of counterfactuals does not force us to accept a new ideology.

Sadly, the many advantages of extreme modal realism come at a heavy price. In the next few sections we shall see that the ontological price of Lewis's theory is extreme. I also urge that one of the supposed outstanding theoretical advantages of the theory, the fact that it is able to provide a reductive analysis of modality, is in fact not true of extreme modal realism.

The incredulous stare

Lewis complained that when he first advocated extreme realism he was not met with argument but with incredulous stares.[13] Nevertheless, as he admits, the incredulous stare is damaging.

The incredulous stare is essentially an expression of the fact that Lewis's brand of modal realism conflicts with common sense. As Lewis grants, a conflict with common sense is not something that can simply be ignored. For Lewis, the philosopher's job is not to justify or undermine our opinions; rather, its job is to systematize these opinions. Usually, in the course of such of a systematization, some of our pre-existing opinions must be altered: some things we thought were true must be counted false, and vice versa. The systematization is a good one as long as it respects those pre-philosophical opinions to which we were firmly attached. Violating these opinions counts against that theory. Thus Lewis admits that its conflict with common sense is a reason for rejecting his theory.

As we have seen, Lewis's theory does well in systematizing and analysing modality. Whether or not to accept his theory is a matter of weighing and balancing; its conflict with common sense must be balanced against its great powers of systematization. Lewis believes that its pros outweigh its cons, and thus he accepts the theory. But stop for a moment and consider the radical damage Lewis's theory does to our common-sense beliefs. I do not believe in unicorns, I do not believe in chimeras, I do not believe in Little Red Riding Hood, and there are countless other possible objects whose existence I do not believe in. But were I to accept Lewis's theory of possible worlds, I would have to reject all these firmly held beliefs. For all its successes, it really is very hard to accept Lewis's theory.

Missing possibilities?

Lewis claims that extreme realism does a good job of systematizing our pre-theoretic modal beliefs. In this section, I argue that there are certain natural beliefs about possibilities that extreme realism is unable to accommodate: certain possibilities are *missing*.

It is plausible to think that there might have been nothing. We think of most objects as existing merely contingently. This computer, this table, this house and this country – each of these things might not have existed. It is plausible to extend this thought and suppose that *none* of these objects could have existed.[14] And some would go even further and argue that there might have been *nothing* at all. Unfortunately, this is not a possibility that the extreme realist can admit. For the extreme realist, possible worlds are maximal spatiotemporally interrelated sums of possible objects. But the mereological sum of nothing isn't anything at all! So there's no such possible world. The extreme modal realist is unable to admit the possibility that there be nothing.

However, independently of extreme modal realism, a number of philosophers deny that there could have been nothing, for they believe in the existence of necessary beings: objects that *must* exist. God, numbers and Platonic properties are all objects that some philosophers have thought must exist necessarily. Is the extreme realist off the hook? No. None of these necessarily existing objects is located in space and time: there are no spatiotemporally extended objects that exist necessarily. Accordingly, we might again think it plausible to move from this to the thought that there could have been no spatiotemporally existing objects, and to believe this without taking sides on the modal status of the existence of Gods or numbers or Platonic properties.

Unfortunately, even the weaker thesis that there might have been no spatiotemporally extended entities is not a possibility that the extreme realist can easily accommodate. As before, possible worlds are mereological sums of maximal *spatiotemporally* related objects. It follows that at every possible world there is at least one spatiotemporally extended object. So the extreme realist must deny that there could have been no spatiotemporally extended entities.

Along similar lines, it is plausible to think that there are worlds that contain a number of disconnected space-times. Not only is this possibility intuitively plausible, but a number of philosophers have argued that it is indeed a genuine possibility. In the course of showing that the identity of indiscernibles is not a necessary truth, Broad argued that spatiotemporal systems entirely cut off from each other are a logical possibility.[15] Some scientists have even suggested that this possibility is in fact realized: that the actual world *does* consist of many disconnected space-times. But this is a possibility that Lewis cannot acknowledge, for Lewis believes that if any two entities are not spatiotemporally related then they are not part of the same possible world. Thus, for any world, all the objects that exist at that world are spatiotemporally related. Therefore there are no worlds that contain disconnected space-times.

Unacceptable ontological extravagance

One obvious criticism of extreme realism is that it is not ontologically parsimonious. The plurality of distinct possible worlds that Lewis postulates to represent every way the world could be is a large plurality indeed.

Lewis has countered this criticism by asking us to distinguish between two types of parsimony: quantitative and qualitative.[16] A theory is quantitatively parsimonious if it is economical in the number of instances of a particular kind of entity it postulates. Thus a theory that postulated only 10^{30} electrons is more quantitatively parsimonious than a theory that postulates 10^{40} electrons. A theory is qualitatively parsimonious if it is economical in the number of different kinds of entities it postulates. Thus a theory that postulates only individuals is more qualitatively parsimonious than one that postulates both individuals and universals. Lewis admits that qualitative parsimony is good in philosophical or empirical theories, but sees no presumption in favour of theories that are quantitatively parsimonious. Lewis claims that his realism about possible worlds is only quantitatively unparsimonious. We already believe in one concrete actual world. Lewis asks us only to believe in more things of the same kind.

We may take issue with the view that there is no presumption in favour of theories that are merely quantitatively parsimonious. We might think that a set-theory, such as ZF minus the axiom of infinity, which is committed to only a countable number of sets, is preferable to ZF with the axiom of infinity, since the latter is committed to an uncountable number of sets. And that ZF is in turn better than ZF plus some large cardinal axiom, again because it postulates fewer sets. Yet each of these theories is as qualitatively parsimonious as any other.

Even if we side with Lewis and favour only qualitative parsimony, still Lewis's argument is flawed, for Lewis not only believes in worlds other than the actual world, but he believes in the possible objects that are parts of these other worlds. And many of these objects *are* qualitatively different from the objects that exist at the actual world. Thus Lewis believes in talking donkeys, philosophizing cats, unicorns, ghosts, spirits, gods and so on – indeed, in any possible *kind* of thing. And since Lewis believes in every possible kind of thing, Lewis's theory is extremely *qualitatively* unparsimonious. This is a massive price to pay, whatever the ideological and analytic benefits of the overall theory.

Primitive modality in extreme realism[17]

One of the advantages of extreme realism is supposed to be that it provides us with an *analysis* of possibility. Few other theories of possible worlds offer to do this. In this section, we shall see that, as a matter of fact, the theory must take modality as primitive to characterize the *set* of possible worlds.

Extreme realism offers an analysis of possibility through the following biconditional:

It is possible that *P* iff there is a world at which P is true

where the left-hand side is understood as being *defined* in terms of the right-hand side.

Now, if we are to accept principle (P) as an analysis of the concept of *possibility* then, at the very least, we have to believe that the principle is extensionally correct. That is, if *P* really is impossible then the extreme realist had better not postulate any maximally spatiotemporally related mereological sums where *P* is true. Similarly, if *P* is possible, then there had better be a maximally spatiotemporally interrelated mereological sum where *P* is true. Unless the theory secures this, there is no reason to think that (P) is even extensionally correct, and thus no reason to accept the analysis. However, all the extreme realist has said so far about possible worlds is that they are maximally spatiotemporally related mereological sums. *This* is quite compatible with there being only three possible worlds, two possible worlds or even just one possible world. This will not do. If it is compatible with the extreme realist's notion of a world that there be just three or four possible worlds, then we have no reason to think that possibility can be analysed in terms of truth at *some* world, or necessity as truth at *all* worlds. Unless the theory postulates a large and varied enough set of possible worlds, we have no reason to think that □ and ◊ should be analysed in terms of truth at all and some of the worlds respectively.

Lewis admits this point and agrees that, for such analyses in terms of the maximally interrelated spatiotemporally mereological sums to be extensionally correct (which is the very least they must be if we are to accept the analysis), the extreme realist must ensure that there are "enough" worlds: that, as Lewis puts it, "there are no gaps in logical space".[18] Let us call a set of worlds that has this property *complete*. How is the extreme realist to ensure that completeness holds?

There is one obvious way to do this. Simply add the principle that if *P* is possible then there is a world at which *P* is true. This will ensure that there are enough mereological sums. But the drawback is obvious: the principle takes the concept of possibility as a primitive. If we add *this* principle to our theory, then we ruin our ability to provide a non-circular analysis of □ and ◊. We need to find another, non-modal way of doing this. How can this be done?

Plenitude

Lewis has suggested that, to achieve his aim, the extreme realist appeal to the Humean denial of necessary connections between distinct existences: the principle of recombination. Intuitively, this principle says that any distinct things may coexist together or fail to coexist together, as long as they occupy distinct spatiotemporal positions. As a first attempt at formalizing this principle, we might write:

> For any set *d* of possible objects there is a world that contains all those objects and those objects occupy different spatiotemporal positions; and, for any subset *g* of *d*, there is a world that contains precisely the members of *g*.

Since objects exist at one world and one world only, this formulation cannot be quite correct. Normally Lewis replaces transworld identity by counterparts but, as he points out, he cannot do this here.[19] What makes one object a counterpart of another may have little to do with the intrinsic nature of the two objects and a lot to do with their surroundings. For instance, it might be that nothing counts as a counterpart of a dragon unless a large part of its surroundings are similar to the dragon's world. Similarly, it might be that nothing is a counterpart of a unicorn unless a large part of its surroundings are similar to the unicorn's world. And it might be that there is no world that matches both the dragon's and the unicorn's world well enough, and so no world contains counterparts of both a dragon and a unicorn:

> Considered by themselves, the dragon and the unicorn are compossible. But if we use the method of counterparts, we do not consider them by themselves; to the extent that the counterpart relation heeds extrinsic similarities, we take them together with their surroundings.[20]

So the principle of recombination must be reformulated using the notion of *duplicates*, where *a* is a duplicate of *b* iff *a* and *b* share all their intrinsic properties. The principle of recombination thus becomes:

> For any set *d* of possible objects there is a world that contains duplicates of all those objects, and, for any subset *g* of *d*, there is a world that contains duplicates of the members of *g* and no other members of *g*.

The possibility of alien properties

The principle of recombination suffices to generate a vast set of worlds according to which all sorts of non-actual possibilities are realized – the existence of talking donkeys, walking centaurs and stalking monsters – indeed, any world instantiating only properties that can be constructed from actually instantiated ones. But even so, the principle still falls short of completeness. There could have been properties that were wholly alien to this world, properties that are not instantiated by any actual object, nor analysable as a conjunctive or structural property built up from constituents that are all instantiated by parts of this world.

Note that an alien property is not just a property that isn't actually instantiated. For instance, the property of *being a unicorn* isn't actually instantiated, but it is not an *alien* property. To be a unicorn is to have certain parts that instantiate certain properties, and to have those parts arranged in a distinctive way. The properties instantiated by the parts, such as *being hooves*, *having blood* or *being wings*, are instantiated in the actual world. The spatial relations between these parts are also instantiated in the actual world. Accordingly, although the property of *being a unicorn* is not actually instantiated, it is not so foreign either; in a sense, it can be constructed or analysed out of properties that *are* actually instantiated. By contrast, an alien property *cannot* be so constructed. Alien properties are *so* foreign to the actual world that we cannot analyse them in terms of actually instantiated properties.

Whereas it is easy to give examples of properties that are non-actual, it is not easy to give examples of properties that are alien. Indeed, the fact that such properties cannot be analysed in terms of actually instantiated ones makes it almost impossible to talk about them. Accordingly, we might wonder whether we really ought to admit that there might have been properties that were alien to the actual world. If these things are ineffable, then do we really do any harm by barring them from our theory of possibility?

Although there are those who believe that alien properties are not possible, this is a minority view. The best way to appreciate the possibility of alien properties is to consider them by analogy. Consider a possible world *w* that is considerably simpler than our own. Whereas our world contains things that instantiate various masses and charges (and yet other esoteric properties such as charm and strangeness), things might not have been so. The world might have been fundamentally Newtonian, containing only bodies that had a Newtonian mass obeying Newton's laws of motion and gravitation. In such a world, the properties of charge and charm would be utterly alien. There is no way of analysing or constructing these properties by rearranging things that only instantiate Newtonian mass. So, from *w*'s point of view, properties such as charge and charm are not just non-actual: they are alien to that world. Accordingly, no matter how we rearrange and patch together various duplicates of the entities that exist at *w*, we have no way of generating a world that contains charged or charmed particles.

What reason do we have to think that *our* world is not in an analogous situation to *w*? After all, the laws of physics are contingent. Whatever physics uncovers, it was always metaphysically possible that things could have been different, and that fundamental particles, instantiating properties that are wholly alien to the actual world, could have been uncovered. Such fundamental properties are *alien* to this world: the very fact that they are *fundamental* implies that they cannot be constituted or analysed in terms of properties that are actually instantiated. Accordingly, if we really wish to respect the metaphysical contingency of fundamental physics, we had better allow that there are such possibilities.

As soon as we allow that there are such possibilities, we immediately see that extreme modal realism, in its current form, is incomplete, for the principle of recombination, as it currently stands, does not entail that there are worlds containing alien properties. Accordingly, completeness has not yet been secured. Nevertheless, it seems an easy matter to plug the gap. Indeed, the very statement of the problem appears to provide the solution. All we need do is supplement the principle of recombination with a postulate saying that there *are* worlds where alien properties are instantiated. So, for instance, we might add to our theory the following principle:

(A) There is at least one world in which there is an individual that instantiates a natural property that is alien to the actual world.

Have we done it? By so supplementing the principle of recombination do we arrive at a theory that has managed to secure completeness in a non-modal manner? Since (A) contains no modal primitives, either hidden or explicit, it is plausible that our theory remains free of modal primitives. But is (A) enough to secure completeness?

Arguably, it is not. After all, for all that has been said so far, it is still consistent that there is only *one* possible alien property. But it is extremely plausible that *many* alien properties could have been instantiated, and not just one. Suppose that scientists were to find a collection of particles that, at first sight, appeared to be alike. After some experimentation, it is discovered that some pairs of these particles tend to *attract* each other with a force inversely proportional to the distance between them, while other pairs tend to *repel* each other with a force inversely proportional to the square of the distance between them. No other differences in behaviour can be found among these particles and, for all the scientists can tell, the objects appear to be structureless. Accordingly, in order to explain the regularity, the scientists postulate that the particles instantiate two different fundamental natural properties and that it is the instantiation of such properties that is responsible for the particles' lawlike behaviour. At the very least, the kinds of objects that these scientists have postulated are possible objects (indeed, they might be our very own positive and negative charges). It is also easy to imagine a world containing particles that fall into three classes. As before, any two particles will either repulse each other with a force inversely proportional to the square of the distance between them, or they will attract each other with a force of the same strength. But whereas before it was true that the maximum number of pairwise repulsing particles was two, in this case the number is three. Such behaviour cannot be explained in terms of positive and negative charge alone. Again, at this world, the relevant particles are structureless, so again it is rational to postulate that the particles instantiate *three* different fundamental natural properties, and that these properties are responsible for the particles' lawlike behaviour. There is no need to stop at three: it is possible to imagine a world containing particles that split into n classes, n being the maximum number of pairwise repulsing particles. Any two particles from the same class repulse each other with a force inversely proportional to the distance between them, and any two particles from different classes attract each other with a force of the same strength. As before, it is plausible to say that this world contains n many natural fundamental properties responsible for these particles' behaviour.

This thought-experiment gives us a sequence of worlds containing more and more distinct properties. There is no reason to think that our world contains arbitrarily many primitive properties that behave in the way these particles do. So, eventually, at some point in the chain, we are describing worlds containing natural properties that are alien to the actual world. Since the chain can be extended arbitrarily far, the chain also gives us arbitrarily many primitive properties that are alien to actuality.

This is all very well. But it's also quite clear what the solution to this problem is as well. Axiom (A) turned out to be too tentative, postulating as it does a measly single alien property. What we need is something that postulates an infinite number of them:

(A⁺)   For any n there are n objects that, between them, instantiate n distinct alien properties.

Unfortunately, the theory is still incomplete.

A model-theoretic argument against completeness

Suppose we grant for *reductio ad absurdum* what the extreme realist requires:

(RED)   Extreme realism plus (A⁺) entails that the set of possible worlds is complete.

Let S be the hypothetically complete set of worlds that, by (RED), is entailed to exist by extreme modal realism. Since our theory entails that there are infinitely many α-alien natural properties instantiated across the worlds of S, so there exists a denumerable sequence of alien natural properties: $P_1, P_2, \ldots, P_n$. Consider now the set S^*, which is just like S save that it fails to contain any world in which P_1 is instantiated, it fails to contain any world in which P_3 is instantiated and, indeed, for any n, fails to contain any world in which property P_{2n+1} is instantiated. Unfortunately, all the principles that we have laid down are just as true of the set S^* as they are of S. For instance, (A⁺) is true of S^*. Since the properties $P_2, P_4, \ldots, P_{2n}$ are all instantiated in worlds in S^*, it is still true that, for any n, there are n objects that instantiate n distinct alien properties. Similarly, the principle of recombination is still true of S^*, for there is no way of rearranging duplicates of things in S^* to give us something that instantiates one of the alien properties $P_1, P_3, \ldots, P_{n+1}$, and so applying combinatorial principles to the worlds of S^* simply generates a world that is already in S^*.

But, by construction, S^* is a proper subset of S. Moreover, it is clear that S^* is an incomplete set of worlds, for S^* fails to include the possibility that there could have been things that instantiated P_1, or could have been things that instantiated P_3 and so on. But since it followed from (RED) that S was the complete set of possible worlds, these are genuine possibilities that are not represented by S^*. Since there are genuine possibilities not captured by S^*, S^* is an incomplete set of worlds.

Since we have seen that all the principles of extreme modal realism, plus the principle of recombination, plus (A$^+$) are true of the worlds in S^*, and since S^* is not a complete set of worlds, it follows that this version of extreme modal realism has *failed* to ensure that the set of worlds really is complete. But this is in contradiction with our initial assumption (RED). Thus we have our desired *reductio*.

If this argument is correct, then we have shown that (RED) entails its own negation. This can only mean one thing: (RED) is false. In other words, our augmented version of extreme modal realism has failed to ensure completeness. Accordingly, the extreme realist has failed to ensure the relevant biconditional

$\Diamond P$ iff there is a world at which P is true

As was urged at the beginning, unless the extreme realist can secure this biconditional, he has given us no reason to think his treatment of possibility as truth at a world is even extensionally correct.

Conclusion

Even if the extreme realist is unable to do without primitive modality, it is still true that the theoretical benefits of this theory of modality are enormous. All the benefits of possible worlds semantics, the analyses of our modal thought and talk, the analyses of counterfactuals and the like are all available to the extreme modal realism. Unfortunately, in my view, the massive ontological cost of the theory and the terrible damage it does to our tenets of common sense outweigh these considerable benefits.

Moderate realism

One can be a realist about possible worlds, believe there are such things that exist independently of our thought and talk, without having to accept Lewis's extreme views about their nature. Possible worlds might be abstract or mathematical entities; they might be sets of propositions or maximal uninstantiated properties; they might be like books or pictures. If we could have a metaphysics that included possible worlds but excluded talking donkeys, stalking monsters and the like, we might be able to help ourselves to many or most of the advantages of possible worlds without having to pay an unacceptable ontological price. We call such a realism about possible worlds *moderate realism*.

At first sight, it may seem that moderate realism is a non-starter. How could one accept the existence of possible worlds at which there are talking donkeys while at the same time rejecting the talking donkeys themselves? This question can be answered by distinguishing between two notions: what is true *of* a possible world and what is true *according to* a possible world. Consider, for example, a particular token of Dickens's *Great Expectations*. It is true *of* this book that it contains 724 pages, that it is made of paper and that it weighs under a kilogram. However, it is true *according to* the book that there exists a character called Pip, that Pip got up to some great larks and that Pip's love is unrequited. It goes without saying that the book doesn't need to *contain* such a character for these things to be true according to the book. Now, when a moderate realist says "There is a world w such that P is true at w", he intends the "P is true at w" to be read as "P is true according to w" rather than "P is true of w". The moderate realist is wholly within his right to do this. The term "true at" is part of the philosopher's theoretical apparatus and the philosopher is free to define his terms as he pleases. Of course, any definition can be criticized if it uses obscure or poorly understood terms itself. And, within reasonable limits, the resultant theory of possible worlds had better be faithful to our pre-theoretic modal judgements. But provided his definition avoids these pitfalls there can be no blame attached to the wily moderate realist who chooses to define "P is true at w" as "P is true according to w" rather than "P is true *of* w". This is how the moderate realist can have possible worlds at which a donkey talks without also having the talking donkey.

What is less clear is how and whether the moderate realist can help himself to an ontology of possibilia. As we have seen, possibilia as much as possible worlds play a key role in the various applications of the possible worlds framework. However, unlike possible worlds, it is not clear whether there is anything analogous to the "true at" phrase for possibilia; but the very fact that this phrase can be understood differently by different theorists is what seems to allow for the possibility of a *moderate* realism.

Some moderate realists, the *linguistic realists*, do indeed take possible worlds to be nothing more than a kind of book.[1] Others, the *combinatorialists*, think that possible worlds are abstract set-theoretic constructions from actually existing particulars and properties.[2] Then there are those moderate realists who think that possible worlds are sets of abstract *propositions*.[3] Yet others take them to be maximally consistent *states of affairs*.[4] Others still identify possible worlds with certain maximal but uninstantiated *properties*.[5] But although there appears to be a wide variety of moderate realisms, we must be cautious. The natures of the entities postulated by different moderate realists are themselves subject to debate: one philosopher's *states of affairs* may be another's *propositions*.

Although the details of moderate realism remain to be fixed, we do know that all moderate realists accept the biconditional

$\Diamond P$ iff there is a possible world at which P is true.

It follows that the moderate realist's worlds must be *consistent*: there must be some way of picking out the books, or sets of propositions or the states of affairs, that *could be true*. This task is not trivial. There are, for example, sets of propositions that are *inconsistent* – for instance, any set containing the propositions *Joe is six feet tall* and *Joe is five feet tall* – and the moderate realist must find a way of excluding these. Moreover, the set of worlds of the moderate realist must be *complete*: for any possibility P, there must be a world according to which P is true.[6] This implies that the moderate realist's ontology must contain enough elements to construct the large variety of possible worlds. This task is not trivial either. For instance, it immediately follows that the linguistic realist cannot identify possibilities with the actual concrete books that have been written; after all, there are infinitely many possibilities but only finitely many actual concrete books, so there are simply not enough books to do the job.

The extreme modal realist had a particularly simple explanation of what it is for P to be the case according to a world: *true at* is more or less just *true of*.[7] There are worlds at which there are talking donkeys because there are worlds that literally contain talking donkeys. Obviously, no moderate realist can follow this route so a natural question arises: how do the worlds, or the elements out of which worlds are constructed, represent different truths as holding there? In other words, what is the moderate realist's account of "P is true at w"?

Moderate realists divide into two camps, depending on how they respond to this question. First, there are those who think that some account or definition must be given of "P is true at w". For instance, linguistic realists take possible worlds to represent in the same way that books do. Some linguistic realists may even try to *define* "P is true at w". Other realists take possible worlds to be like pictures, and think that they represent in the same way that pictures do: by the existence of some shared structure between the picture and that which is represented. Secondly, there are those who think that, at the most fundamental level, there is nothing much that can be said, or that needs to be said, about how possible worlds or their elements manage to represent properties. Such moderate realists are simply *quiet* about the notion of truth at a world. All the quiet moderate realist needs is for there to be sufficiently many entities capable of representing all the different possibilities; it's enough that there are these things that have these representational properties, and no account of the nature of these properties needs to be given. On this view, the phrase "is true at" is essentially a *primitive* of the theory. We call realists who take this latter course *quiet* moderate realists. At a fundamental level, such realists refuse to say how their basic entities represent.

Lewis's *ontology* is criticized not just for being unparsimonious, but also for being downright implausible. We might equally well criticize the quiet moderate realist's *ideology* as downright implausible too. While notions of fundamental properties and relations might plausibly be taken as primitive, it seems very strange that the predicate "is true at" should be taken as a primitive; it seems to beg analysis. Similarly, one wonders whether the relation *is true of* is also supposed to be a primitive relation; this, again, would be very strange, seeming as it does to postulate primitive, irreducible semantic facts. There is a suspicion here that, at the very outset, the quiet moderate realist has helped himself to all the advantages of theft over honest toil.

However, we shall presently grant the quiet moderate realist his primitives and examine his position. Since there are many varieties of quiet moderate realism, we will focus on three versions that have been particularly well developed: the view that worlds are sets of propositions; the view that worlds are states of affairs; and the view that worlds are recombinations of the objects and properties that exist or are instantiated at the actual world.

Possible worlds as sets of propositions

It is the moderate realist's aim to build possible worlds out of what he regards as a safe and sane ontology. The hope is that, by using entities that we have prior reasons for believing in, or entities that do little damage to our ordinary thought and talk, we will be able to generate things that are capable of doing all or most of the useful work that possible worlds can do without incurring an unacceptable philosophical cost. The moderate realist wishes to avoid the damage that extreme realism does to common sense, and avoid its extravagant ontology. Accordingly, the moderate realist will try to show how we can construct possible worlds from entities that are unproblematic, either because they are part of our common-sense ontology, or because of the useful theoretical role they play in explaining some other feature of the world.

With this in mind, those who identify possible worlds with sets of propositions might motivate their views as follows. First, they might tell us that it is natural to believe in propositions for much the same reason as it is natural to believe in worlds. In our everyday thought and talk we make many claims that commit us to there being such things. For instance, it is natural to say that the sentences "Snow is white" and "La neige est blanche" both express the same proposition. If you believe that the earth is square and I believe the earth is square then it is natural to say that there is some proposition that we both believe in. And most of us believe that there are certain propositions whose truth-value we may never uncover.

In our philosophical theorizing, propositions are thought to play an important role in the philosophy of mind. One of the central questions in the philosophy of mind is this: given that we are nothing more than mere physical devices, nothing more than complicated and finely honed parts of natural the world, how do our mental states manage to be *about* things – how do our thoughts, beliefs and desires come to have a particular content? And workers in the philosophy of mind have typically framed this issue using the notion of a *proposition*. The question is typically expressed: how, as mere physical objects, are we capable of standing in certain relations to a proposition?

(Of course, these comments are intended only to indicate why the view that there are propositions might have some plausibility, or why the postulation of propositions might have some theoretical utility, independently of any considerations about modality. These are not meant to be watertight arguments. Needless to say, any hypothesis according to which there is an infinity of abstract entities is going to have its critics.[8])

If we already accept propositions in our ontology then maybe we can take possible worlds to be constructed from them. Clearly, possible worlds cannot be *identified* with propositions. After all, certain propositions, such as "Joe weighs twelve stone and also weighs thirteen stone" describe *impossibilities*. Similarly, certain propositions are *incomplete*. The proposition "There is something that is red and there is something that is green" is true in many different possible situations. Nothing is said about the number of objects that exist, or the other properties that the red thing and the green thing might have. But possible worlds are typically thought of as being a *complete* way in which things could have been.[9] The solution is to identify possible worlds with certain *sets* of propositions. The sets that we need are the *maximally consistent* sets of propositions. A set of propositions is *consistent* if the members of the set *could* all be true together. This ensures that all the worlds will indeed be *possible* worlds. A set S of propositions is maximal if, were any other proposition to be added to S, the set would become *inconsistent*. Similarly, it had better be part of our conception of proposition to ensure that, for *any* possibility, there is a proposition or set of propositions according to which that possibility holds. Finally, a proposition P is true at a world iff P is a member of that world.

Given this machinery, we recover the desired biconditional:

$\Diamond P$ iff P is true at some possible world.

But what are the costs and the benefits of such a theory of possible worlds?

We judge the economy of a theory by examining the number of kinds of entities the theory introduces, and the number of predicates the theory takes as primitive. True, this theory introduces an infinity of propositions, but it is qualitative, not quantitative, parsimony that matters. Here, the theory might be said to have postulated just the one *type* of entity: *proposition*. In comparison to the ontological extravagance of the extreme realist's theory, this may strike us as far more ontologically parsimonious. However, the theorist has told us nothing about the nature of these propositions. It may be that all propositions are, intrinsically, exactly alike, in which case the theory has indeed introduced only one new kind of entity. But maybe propositions are not all alike. Maybe the proposition "There are protons" is qualitatively different from the proposition "There are electrons"; after all, protons themselves are qualitatively different from electrons. Unfortunately, we have been told so little about propositions that it is impossible to tell whether two distinct propositions are qualitatively different. Until a little more is said about the nature of propositions, it is hard to say just how ontologically parsimonious the theory is.

How does the view that worlds are sets of propositions fare when we come to judge its ideological economy? What are the *primitives* of the theory? Of course, unless some kind of reductive theory of propositions is forthcoming, the theory first takes the predicate "... is a proposition" as a primitive. Secondly, the theory takes the notion "is true at" as a primitive. Thirdly, since worlds are maximally consistent *sets* of propositions, the theory also takes the predicate "... is a set" as a primitive. Fourthly, *necessity* (or *possibility*) must also be taken as a primitive. Possible worlds have been defined as *maximally consistent* sets of propositions. *Maximal consistency* uses modality twice over. *Consistency* itself is a modal notion: a set of propositions is consistent iff all the members of the set *could* all be true together. The set *S* is maximal if every set that properly includes *S could not* be true together. So the notion of possibility itself is a primitive of the theory. This clearly rules out any chance of a reductive analysis of modality from the outset.

As far as the ideological economy goes, then, the theory appears to be more extravagant than extreme realism. However, at first sight it seems a reasonable price to pay. True, the notion of possibility – a notion that the extreme realist hopes to do without – is primitive; true also, the notion of a proposition – a notion which was not needed in extreme realism – is primitive. But perhaps a few new primitives do not seem such a great price to pay to reap the benefits of possible worlds while avoiding the madness of extreme realism.[10] Again, though, one can wonder about whether these primitives are *reasonable* primitives. After all, haven't the semantic paradoxes shown that our intuitive notion of a proposition is not particularly clear, that propositions themselves are entities that call for philosophical clarification and analysis? Yet here we find them being taken as primitives of the theory.

Worse, the moderate realism sketched here gives us few of the theoretical benefits typically associated with possible worlds.

For all that has been said so far, this theory does not even give us possible worlds semantics – at least, if we want a possible worlds semantics for quantified modal logic. True, this quiet moderate realism gives us a set of possible worlds, and it has given us a notion of what it is for a proposition to be true at a world. This much would suffice to justify the model theory for *propositional* modal logic. But remember that the models for QML have more structure than this. Recall that these models also include a place for the *set of all possible individuals*, and this set plays an apparently indispensable role in giving the semantics for our quantified modal sentences.

On the theory of possible worlds currently under consideration, *no provision for this set has been made*. All that we have so far is a set of possible worlds according to which various things are the case. It is not easy to see how this version of quiet moderate realism is to be extended to provide for a set of possible individuals.

The lack of a set of possible individuals also gives rise to problems for the analytic ambitions of this theory, because possible worlds analyses of certain modal sentences that could not be expressed in QML are no longer available. Recall that QML had difficulties expressing: (i) numerical quantification over possibilities; (ii) sentences comparing the sizes of different domains; and (iii) modalized comparatives. While the view that worlds are sets of propositions can accommodate (i) – let such quantification be understood as over *sets* of possible worlds – the theory is unable to deal with (ii) and (iii). Recall the sentence "There could have been more things than there actually are." In possible worlds terms, this sentence is analysed as "There is a world whose domain includes the domain of the actual world." Without possible individuals in our ontology, as well as the possible worlds, we are still left with no way to analyse this sentence. As for (iii), recall that the extreme realist's analysis of "My car could have been the same colour as your car actually is" is "There is a counterpart of my car that is the same colour as your car." But without possibilia to play with, the quiet moderate realist again lacks the means to analyse this sentence in his framework.

What of the other analytic ambitions of this theory? Consider, for instance, the analysis of counterfactuals. Recall that, on the possible worlds analysis, the counterfactual "If *A* were the case then *B* would be the case" is true precisely when *B* is true at the closest world where *A* is true. But what does "closest" mean in this context? For the extreme realist, closeness is nothing more than the familiar relation of similarity. But what can our moderate realist take this relation to be? Are we to think of *propositions* as being similar or dissimilar to each other? Again, I complain that we have been told so little about the nature of propositions that, for all that has been said so far, two entirely different propositions may be exactly alike. True, the realist might postulate a primitive relation *R* holding between different worlds, and use this relation as a measure of the closeness to analyse counterfactuals. But postulating one new primitive relation in order to analyse the notion of counterfactuals results in no overall increase of theoretical economy. The number of primitives remains the same in the two cases.

I don't say that these problems are insurmountable. There may be ways of developing this realism that overcome these difficulties. But the work is there to do. Until such developments are forthcoming, the analytic ambitions of the theory are severely limited. Until then, it is hard to see what there is to recommend such a theory. What's the point of accepting possible worlds into our ontology if they do virtually no philosophical work?

Possible worlds as states of affairs

Plantinga has done more than anyone to develop and defend the view that possible worlds are certain states of affairs.[11] In certain respects, his theory resembles the view that possible worlds are sets of propositions but, as we shall see, Plantinga has a far more sophisticated theory than the one sketched above.

The basic building blocks of Plantinga's theory are *states of affairs*. As with propositions, defenders of states of affairs might try to motivate their existence on grounds independent of modality. Such defenders might tell us that it is natural to believe in states of affairs because, in our everyday thought and talk, we make various claims that commit us to such things. For instance, we might talk of a particular state of affairs as being interesting, or being important; we might say that one state of affairs causes or is caused by some other state of affairs; or we might want to know what brought about a particular state affairs. Some might say their existence is just plausible: "it is obvious, I think, that there are such things as states of affairs: for example, *Quine's being a philosopher*".[12] And, indeed, when the point is put this way, it does appear obvious that Quine's being a philosopher is one of many states of affairs.

Besides common sense, states of affairs seem to play a role in our philosophical theorizing. Some philosophers have used the notion of a state of affairs in their analysis of causation. Others think that states of affairs play a useful role in giving content to the truth-maker principle, which states that, for any truth, there is something in the world that *makes* that proposition true, something whose mere existence *entails* the truth of that proposition. For truth-maker theorists, the things that make propositions true are certain states of affairs. However, we must be very careful here. For it is not at all clear that the kinds of things that make truths true, or that play a role in our analysis of causation, are the same things that moderate realists need for their theory of possible worlds. Different theorists may mean quite different things by the words "states of affairs". To understand why, we must develop the view that possible worlds are states of affairs a little further.

All the "obvious" examples of states of affairs that come to mind, states of affairs such as *Quine's being a philosopher*, *Blair's being prime minister*, *(7 + 5)'s being 12*, are things that we might also call "truths". I acknowledge that it is natural and intuitive to move from "it's a truth that *P*" to "it's a state of affairs that *P*". However, if we wish to construct possible worlds out of states of affairs then, quite clearly, the states of affairs will have to *outnumber* the truths. We will have to postulate states of affairs that are *not* truths. After all, *Quine's being a philosopher* may indeed be a state of affairs. But it is possible that Quine could have been a politician and there is no obvious way to construct the relevant possible world out of the truths about Quine. Accordingly, those who would construct worlds out of states of affairs also claim that *Quine's being a politician* and *Bush's being a philosopher* are states of affairs. Both *Quine's being a philosopher* and *Quine's being a politician* exist, both are equally much part of the ontology of the world as each other, both are existing states of affairs.

What's going on? We began with something that appeared obvious, but we are now saying things that seem extremely contentious. How can we say that the state of affairs *Quine's being a politician* exists? After all, Quine is most definitely a philosopher and he's clearly no politician. The trick is to postulate a distinction between different kinds of states of affairs. All kinds of states of affairs *exist*, but only some kinds of states of affairs *obtain*. *Quine's being a philosopher* and *Bush's being a politician* are both states of affairs that *obtain*, while *Quine's being a politician* and *Bush's being a philosopher* are states of affairs that do not *obtain*. Yet all of these states of affairs *exist*. Armed with non-obtaining states of affairs, we are able to develop a theory of possible worlds not unlike the theory of the previous section, where worlds were identified with sets of propositions.

As before, not any arbitrary state of affairs qualifies as a possible world. *Quine's being a politician* may be a possible state of affairs, but it does not represent a *complete* possible world. Similarly, *(2 + 2)'s being 5* may be a state of affairs, but it is not a *possible* state of affairs and therefore must not be included in any state of affairs that represents a possible world. Accordingly, we need to pick out those states of affairs that are *maximal* and *consistent*. A state of affairs is consistent if it's *possible* that the state of affairs obtain. *Maximal* is explained in the following way. Let us say that a state of affairs *S includes S** if it is not *possible* for *S* to obtain and for *S** not to obtain. A state of affairs *S precludes S** if it is not possible that *S* obtains and *S** obtains. A maximal state of affairs is one that includes or precludes every other state of affairs. The possible worlds are exactly those states of affairs that are maximal and consistent.

First, let's note the cost in terms of ideological economy of this version of quiet moderate realism. As well as taking the predicate "is a state of affairs" as primitive, the theory also has introduced the primitive predicate "obtains". Possible worlds are states of affairs that are maximal and consistent. Both these notions are eventually defined in terms of *possibility* so, like the theory that worlds are sets of propositions, the "possibly" is one of the primitives of the theory. Again, there is no hope here for carrying out a reductive analysis of modality.

What of the prior plausibility of the entities postulated? I believe that it is low. While it may be natural to say that there is such a state of affairs as *Quine's being a philosopher*, it is not nearly as natural to say that *Quine's being a politician* is a state of affairs. Indeed, precisely because he is not a politician I am inclined to say that this is not a state of affairs at all. True, in some contexts, *states of affairs* seem to be reasonably familiar things. Whilst a state of affairs may not quite be the kind of thing you can spill your coffee over, the view that the world is a world of states of affairs rather than a world of things has some plausibility. In that sense, the state of affairs of *Quine's being a philosopher* seems to be a reasonably attractive kind of entity, one with which we might plausibly claim to have some kind of familiarity.[13] But how do states of affairs such as *Quine's being a politician* fit into this picture? The kinds of states of affairs needed to construct possible worlds are generally taken to be *abstract entities*, entities standing outside space and time, entities that have no causal powers. I, for one, do not associate my everyday conception of states of affairs with such entities. Far from being part of our common-sense thought and talk, the kinds of states of affairs needed here turn out to be a philosopher's invention. This does not make for the desired attractive ontology that the quiet moderate realist initially promised us.

What about the theoretical or philosophical roles that states of affairs are supposed to play independently of any considerations in modality? As mentioned above, some philosophers have taken states of affairs to be the *relata* of the causal relation. But if states of affairs are abstract entities, existing outside space and time and devoid of causal power, then it's not at all clear that these things are suited to play this role at all. And it is certainly not true that the states of affairs of the moderate realist can function as Armstrongian *truth-makers* for our ordinary thought and talk, for the truth-maker principle requires that the mere existence of the state of affairs *Quine's being a philosopher* entails that Quine is a philosopher. This does not hold on Plantinga's view. For Plantinga, all kinds of states of affairs exist: merely possible ones as well as ones that correspond to truths. The existence of the state of affairs *Bush's being a philosopher* had better not entail that Bush is a philosopher.

We see that that the theory pays quite a price in terms of the attractiveness of its ontology, and in terms of the predicates and concepts that the theory must take as primitive. What of the analytic ambitions of the theory? As in the previous section above, we can again complain that, in many cases, the theory has not been as well developed as we would like. As before, it's not clear how the analysis of counterfactuals is to be pursued. Recall that to analyse this notion we need not only possible worlds, but also a relation of closeness to hold between them. However, since it's unclear what kinds of intrinsic properties Plantinga's states of affairs have, it's unclear whether we can talk of various states of affairs as being similar to each other – so, unlike in extreme realism, it is not clear that the familiar notion of similarity can do the job here. Perhaps a new primitive of *closeness* is needed to carry out the analysis of counterfactuals, but this is to the detriment of the overall theoretical economy of the theory.

So far the theory actually looks like the view that worlds are propositions. Instead of propositions, we have states of affairs.

Instead of distinguishing between those propositions that are true and those that are false, we distinguish between those states of affairs that obtain and those that do not. And, as with the theory above, states of affairs have merely given us a set of possible worlds. We have nothing to play the part of the possible individuals. And, as we have seen, this places a severe limit on the analytic ambitions of the theory. As we saw above, to justify the use of possible worlds semantics and to analyse the meaning of various modal sentences in English, we need something to play the role of the possible individuals.

However, Plantinga gives the states of affairs theory a new twist: he introduces further elements and primitives into his theory in order to get the effect of quantifying over possibilia. These new elements are the *individual essences*. An individual essence is a property of an individual *a* that is: (i) essential to *a* – *a* could not exist without instantiating that property; (ii) necessarily unique to *a* – necessarily *a* is the only entity that instantiates that property.

What are we to make of individual essences? Note that the postulation of individual essences is stronger than the acceptance of essential properties. You and I might have our *humanity* necessarily, but since this property is shared by both of us, it cannot be an individual essence. One might have thought that, given the widespread disagreement as to whether or not objects even have any of their properties essentially, whether anything instantiates an essence would be a contentious matter. But according to Plantinga, this is mistaken. Consider the property *being identical to Socrates*. This a property that Socrates must instantiate (for Socrates could not exist without being identical to himself) and that *only* Socrates can instantiate (for if any other entity *x* instantiated *being identical to Socrates*, then *x* would be identical to Socrates, and so not another entity after all). Since Plantinga thinks it obvious that there are such properties as *being identical to Socrates*, he thinks it obvious that there are individual essences.

It is individual essences that, on this version of quiet moderate realism, will appear in the domain *D* of the intended interpretation of QML. But for this to be successful, the inductive definition of truth-in-a-model has to be modified. When we say "There could have been more things than there actually are", we cannot treat this as true precisely when there is a world whose domain is a subset of the set of objects that actually exist. This is because Plantinga believes that individual essences are *necessary* existents. Although Socrates may exist contingently, his essence exists necessarily. So exactly the same essences exist at all worlds. Rather, what is meant is that there is some world w such that the essences that are instantiated there are a subset of the essences that are actually instantiated. Similarly, when writing the various clauses for possible worlds semantics we have to be careful to read existential quantification as a way of talking about which essences are instantiated at a world rather than which entities exist at a world.

Although we have a sketch of how the introduction of individual essences gives us a way of making sense of possible worlds semantics, and of paraphrasing certain everyday claims about the various sizes of worlds, it is not clear whether this apparatus can be put to the range of uses that extreme realism can be put to. Consider again the modalized comparative "My car could have been the same colour as your car actually is." The extreme realist can treat this as expressing the familiar *same colour as* relation between a counterpart of my car and your actual car. But how do we proceed if we have individual essences rather than possibilia? The sentence can't be treated as expressing the *same colour as* relation between two individual essences. Like states of affairs, like propositions, it's not clear that essences are the kinds of things that have properties, and it's certainly implausible to think that essences have colours! I don't say that the trick can't be done, but if our theory of possible worlds is to help us analyse and understand such modal claims then we need to see how it is done.

Of more serious worry is the fact that this extra explanatory power has come at some cost to the theoretical and ontological economy of the theory. A new category of entities, *individual essences*, has been introduced, and the new predicate *is exemplified* now forms part of our theory. But is it particularly plausible that there are such things as individual essences? Perhaps it's not so plausible to believe in properties such as *being red* or *being square*. But many would balk at the idea that *being identical to Socrates* is a genuine property.

There is worse to come. The domain D is supposed to be the set of all possible objects. On this picture the sentence "There could have been things that don't actually exist" is true because there exists some individual essence that is not instantiated but that could have been. But what on earth are we to make of properties such as *being identical to* a, when *a* does not exist? Had Socrates not existed then I wouldn't have been inclined to say that the property of being identical to Socrates would have existed either. We may have been suspicious of essences to begin with, but to postulate essences of objects that do not actually exist is, for many, a postulate too far.

Combinatorialism

The fundamental idea that underlies the various versions of combinatorialism is that possible worlds are nothing more than rearrangements or recombinations of the properties, relations and particulars that are instantiated or exist in the actual world. For example, there exists the entity Joe who, as things actually are, instantiates the property *being six feet tall*. There exists the entity Flo who, as things actually are, instantiates the property *being five feet tall*. However, by recombining these elements we can generate an alternative world where Joe instantiates the property *being five feet tall*, and Flo instantiates the property *being six feet tall*. And, in general, if there actually exists some entity *a*, and some property *F* is actually instantiated, then we can form the possibility of *a*'s being *F*.

Of course, the combinatorialist must give an account of the ontology of combinations. The combinatorialist insight tells us something about the nature of possibility, but if the combinatorialist desires a theory of possible worlds, and wants to help himself to the many advantages the theory has provided, then he needs to say just what things these possible worlds are. Fortunately, by appealing to set theory, there is a natural way of developing the combinatorialist's story. A simple recombination can be identified with an *ordered n-tuple* consisting of an actually instantiated property and $n - 1$ actual particulars. Thus, given that *a* and *b* exist, and that the property *F* and the two-place relation *R* are actually instantiated, the six simple recombinations that can be made from these elements can be identified with the ordered *n*-tuples $<F, a>$, $<F, b>$, $<R, a, a>$, $<R, a, b>$, $<R, b, a>$ and $<R, b, b>$. Possible worlds can then be identified with *sets* of these *n*-tuples. Where an *n*-tuple is a member of *w*, that recombination obtains at that world;

where an n-tuple is not a member of w, that recombination does not obtain at that world. Note, though, that this means that the combinatorialist must treat properties with ontological seriousness, so there is some cost here to ontological parsimony. How attractive an ontology of properties is will depend upon the details of combinatorialism. In Chapter 7, we will develop the position further, and show that there are reasons for optimism: the combinatorialist has available to him a fairly attractive theory of properties.

An example illustrates the combinatorialist's idea. Let w be the set $\{<F, a>, <R, a, b>\}$. According to w, a instantiates F while b does not. Moreover, a bears R to b while b does not bear R to a. Nor does any object bear R to itself.

For the combinatorialist, a possible world is nothing more than a recombination of properties and particulars. We might expect the combinatorialist to follow the template set by other moderate realists and restrict the possible worlds to those recombinations that are *consistent*; unfortunately, to the detriment of the theory's ideological economy, this means taking modality as primitive. However, the combinatorialist can here urge that it is in the nature of modality that any recombination of *distinct* properties and particulars *will* result in a genuine possibility. If such a principle of recombination is right, then the combinatorialist can spell out his theory without using primitive modality.

In Chapter 5, we saw that one extreme realist, Lewis, accepts the principle of recombination. So is Lewis a combinatorialist? No. We must distinguish principles of recombination, which tell us only something about the range and variety of possible worlds, and combinatorialism, which, at least as it is to be understood here, also tells us something about the metaphysical nature of possible worlds themselves. So, for instance, one could accept a principle of recombination on which, if there is a world at which there is an x that instantiates an intrinsic property F, and if there is a world at which there is a y that instantiates an intrinsic property G, then there is a world at which there is an x that is F and a y that is G. But this principle alone is completely neutral about the nature of possible worlds. Accepting a principle of recombination does not automatically make one a combinatorialist.

Of course, principles of recombination do lie at the heart of the combinatorialist's position. But the combinatorialist's version of the principle may be quite different from the principles of recombination accepted by Lewis. For Lewis, recombination is a matter of taking *duplicates* of different parts of worlds and then pasting those duplicates together in various ways to form new possible worlds. For the combinatorialist, recombination is a matter of taking the particulars and properties instantiated by the actual world and rearranging them and, on a natural and intuitive way of understanding this principle, it entails the existence of worlds that the Lewisian principle of recombination does not. This is shown as follows. Consider a simple world w that contains just two objects, a and b, and suppose that the only qualitative property instantiated by a is F and the only qualitative property instantiated by b is G. By recombining the particulars and the properties we can generate another possible world w^* that also just contains a and b, but where a is G and b is F. But note that worlds w and w^* are qualitatively indiscernible. Even God, looking down, would not notice the difference between the two. Similarly, we can recombine the elements of the actual world to form a possible world where I have all of your properties and you have all of mine. Again, this construction generates two worlds that differ only over which objects have which properties.[14] By contrast, the extreme realist's principle of recombination, which works with *duplicates*, does not generate distinct but qualitatively identical worlds: given world w, the principle will tell us that there is a world containing a duplicate of a and a duplicate of b, but not that there is a world at which a has G's properties and vice versa.

From an ontological point of view, combinatorialism promises the most of all the quiet moderate realisms so far examined, for the combinatorialist's worlds can be taken to be nothing more than set-theoretic constructions from actually existing particulars and actually instantiated properties – an ontology that many philosophers have found to be plausible independently of any considerations from modality. But despite the theory's attractive ontology, there are questions about the number of theoretical benefits this version of realism can deliver. Again, the theory does not serve up possibilia, and this deprives us of the straightforward explanation of the appropriateness of possible worlds semantics. As before, the current theory has no difficulties dealing with our numerical quantification over possibilities, but statements such as "There could have been more things than there actually are" and "My car could have been the same colour as your car actually is" are not obviously analysable given the resources of this version of realism. Besides these familiar limitations, there are also two problems that are particular to combinatorialism.

1. *The problem of incompatible properties.* Objects cannot simultaneously have different determinate properties of the same determinable. For instance, an object cannot simultaneously be red and green. Yet, just as we can reshuffle the particulars and properties of the actual world to form a rearrangement according to which snow is green and the sky is white, and a rearrangement according to which I am five feet tall and hirsute, so we can reshuffle the particulars and properties of the actual world to form a rearrangement according to which grass is red and green. Accordingly, it seems as if the concept of a recombination goes *beyond* the concept of what is possible: there are recombinations of elements of the actual world that do not correspond to possibilities.

   Clearly, the combinatorialist's world-making principles must be restricted. The obvious way to restrict the principle is to say that possible worlds are those recombinations that do not ascribe incompatible properties to one and the same object. The drawback here is that the restriction uses primitive modality: two properties are incompatible if they *could* not both be instantiated by one and the same object.[15] Should the combinatorialist help himself to this solution, he will be unable to provide a non-circular analysis of the notion of possibility.

2. *The problem of alien particulars and properties.* This difficulty arises precisely because the combinatorialist has tried to keep to an attractive ontology of actual particulars and actually instantiated universals. Intuitively, it is possible that there could have existed something that was *wholly new* to the actual world. There might have been a brand new entity, which was not identical to any actually existing thing. Similarly, there might have been alien properties, properties so foreign to actuality that they could not be analysed in terms of properties that were actually instantiated. But there is no way of recombining the elements of the actual world to make a world that contains

entities that are so alien to actuality. Accordingly, it seems as if the concept of a recombination *falls short* of what is possible: there are possibilities that do not correspond to any recombination.

Problem 1 might be solved by restricting the combinatorialist principle, albeit at the expense of our analytic ambitions. But problem 2 is far more serious for the combinatorialist. Since there are possibilities that do not correspond to any recombination, no *restriction* of the combinatorialist principle is going to help us here. The only way of *extending* the principle would be to allow recombination over both actual and *non-actual* particulars and properties. But once the combinatorialist finds himself postulating non-actual entities his theory immediately becomes as implausible and counter-intuitive as genuine modal realism. Indeed, the whole point of the moderate realist's enterprise is to find a theory of possible worlds that *avoids* having to postulate non-actual entities.

Some combinatorialists have simply bitten the bullet and declared that it is *impossible* that there be alien properties or particulars.[16] But this seems a desperate measure. We have already seen that there were very strong reasons for accepting that there could have been properties that were alien to actuality. And the view that there could have been *more* things than there actually are seems to be a firm modal intuition. If we are wrong about *that* then it's not clear which of our modal views we can hold with any confidence at all.

The return of the incredulous stare

Extreme realism is often met with an incredulous stare, and quite rightly so. Quiet moderate realism is not. It should be. Although there are differences between the moderate realisms sketched above, there are clear similarities. Indeed, it's not hard to discern a blueprint for generating realisms here. The names may change but the story is always the same. So, for instance, say that there exists a collection of *circumstances*, or *situations*, or *natures*, or *incidents* ... (you should use your own creativity and find some other word to introduce a new brand of entities). Feel free to use these familiar words to give you the illusion that you are doing nothing more than introducing a category of entity that is entirely natural and with which you are entirely familiar. Feel free to ignore all aspects of our ordinary thought and talk of circumstances or situations or natures or incidents that are incompatible with your particular understanding of these entities. Distinguish between those circumstances that *hold* and those that do not, or those situations that *happen* and those that do not, or those *natures* that are instantiated and those that are not, or those incidents that *occur* and those that do not. Then build up possible worlds as special maximally consistent circumstances, situations, natures and incidents. Feel free to say nothing about the nature of these entities, other than that they all exist and are all abstract and are all actual; feel free to say nothing about the nature of transworld identity; feel free to say nothing about how these entities manage to represent all the possibilities that there could be; feel free not to postulate anything that can do the work of the domain *D*; feel free to say nothing about how these things help with the analysis of our ordinary modal thought and talk, such as sentences comparing the domains of different worlds, modalized comparatives or supervenience claims; feel free to omit the necessary details that would explain how your theory can help us analyse counterfactuals; finally, feel free to claim that the theory has all or most of the benefits associated with a theory of possible worlds and stop right there. And now feel free to feel ashamed of yourself for thinking that the little language game you've set up deserves to be called a *theory* of modality. Anyone offering up such meagre pickings warrants as much of an incredulous stare as the extreme modal realist. *This* is a *theory* of modality?

An argument against quiet moderate realism?

I have tried to show that, although the ontology of the quiet moderate realist may be preferable to the extreme realist's, it is still a long way from being a plausible one. Moreover, quiet moderate realists have much work to do to show that their theories of possible worlds are really able to capture all the theoretical benefits possible worlds can offer. On the cost–benefit analysis, quiet moderate realism is disappointing.

Lewis has developed an *argument* against quiet moderate realism that purports to show that, even setting aside the cost–

benefit analysis, the notions the quiet moderate realist takes as primitive are seriously problematic.[17] In the rest of this chapter, we examine Lewis's argument. We shall find that, although it may force the quiet moderate realist to make certain concessions, the argument is a double-edged sword for Lewis: in so far as there is a version of the argument that works, this argument threatens equally Lewis's overall metaphysical framework.

We begin with some terminology. All quiet moderate realists postulate two basic primitives:

- a set of entities that may be the quiet moderate realist's worlds or that may be used to construct the worlds (so, referring back to the quiet moderate realisms examined so far, these may be the properties, propositions, states of affairs or recombinations) – from hereon, we call whatever entities the quiet moderate realist postulates *elements*
- a relation that holds between the actual world and the primitive entities postulated above (depending upon the choice of theory they say that the actual world *makes true* a certain set of propositions, or that the actual world makes it the case that a certain set of states of affairs *obtains* or that the actual world *instantiates* a certain property) – in this chapter, we call whatever relation the quiet moderate realist postulates the *selection* relation: the actual world *selects* a particular element.

Furthermore, quiet moderate realists accept the following minimal view about the representational properties of the elements: what makes it the case that a particular element *e* represents the existence of a talking donkey is the fact that, necessarily, when the concrete world contains a talking donkey, then (and only then) it selects the element *e*.

Lewis's arguments against quiet moderate realism rest upon a distinction between internal and external relations. An *internal* relation is one that supervenes upon the intrinsic properties of its relata.[18] Thus, if *a* and *b* stand in some internal relation *R*, while *c* and *d* do not, then either the intrinsic natures of *a* and *c* must differ, or the intrinsic natures of *b* and *d* must differ. *Resembles*, *is taller than* and *is smaller than* are all examples of internal relations. In contrast, a relation is *external* iff it is not internal.[19] *Distance* is an example of an external relation.

Lewis's arguments against the quiet moderate realist vary depending upon whether he takes the selection relation to be internal or external. In either case, Lewis thinks the quiet moderate realist is in trouble.[20]

Selection is internal

Suppose that the realist takes the relation of selection as internal:

> when the concrete world selects an element, that is so in virtue of what goes on within the concrete world together with the intrinsic nature of the selected element ... There is one element which, in virtue of its intrinsic nature, necessarily will be selected iff there is a talking donkey within the concrete world.[21]

Hence, if the relation of selection is internal, the intrinsic natures of various elements must vary, for it is in virtue of the intrinsic nature of an element that it is selected iff there is a talking donkey.

We now know that the intrinsic natures of the moderate realist's primitive entities are different; in other words, there are qualitative differences between the different entities. This fact casts doubts upon the claim that quiet moderate realism is more ontologically parsimonious than Lewis's theory, for it undermines the view that the class of elements is only one *kind* of extra entity.

Lewis argues that, if the elements have different natures, it is fair to ask what the elements are like, how it is they differ from one another and what properties they have in virtue of which one of them is selected.[22] The simple response is that some element has the property *representing that a donkey talks*. But this will not do. As Lewis says:

> we have danced a tiny circle: there is an element such that, necessarily, it is selected iff a donkey talks; that element has some distinctive intrinsic property; that property is named "representing that a donkey talks"; the property with that name singles out the element that, necessarily, is selected iff a donkey talks. Not a thing has been said about what sort of property that might be.

He concludes that "we have not the slightest idea what the representational properties are".[23]

Lewis is right: the quiet moderate realist refuses to say anything about his elements, and we have no grasp on the properties that they have by which they do their representational work. Yet it is highly plausible that, in order to understand a predicate for an internal relation R, we must know what features objects a and b possess that enable them to enter into relation R. For if two objects enter into internal relation R, then there is some intrinsic feature of those objects in virtue of which those objects are capable of entering into relation R.[24] Now, to understand a sentence is to know how the world would have to be in order to make it true. Suppose that R is the name of some internal relation. Then the sentence aRb is true in virtue of a particular feature of a and a particular feature of b. But if someone does not know in virtue of what a and b are capable of standing in the relation R, then he cannot claim he knows how things would have to be for aRb to be true.

Indeed, for every internal relation with which we are familiar, it seems absurd to suppose that one could grasp the internal relation without knowing the kinds of properties the relata possess in virtue of which they stand in that relation. Consider, for example, the internal relation *larger than*. In order for an object to be capable of bearing this relation it must have a size. It is impossible that anything that did not possess a size could be larger than another object. And if to grasp an internal relation it is necessary to know in virtue of what an object is capable of bearing this relation, then in order to grasp the relation *larger than* we must possess the concept of size. Anyone who claimed to understand the predicate "x is larger than y" while claiming that he had no grip of the notion of size would be regarded as at best confused, at worst insane.

Taking the selection relation as internal leads to problems. Let us therefore see what happens when the quiet moderate realist takes the relation to be external.

Selection is external

If selection is external then the quiet moderate realist need not give an account of the intrinsic nature of his elements, for, by definition, an external relation does not hold in virtue of the intrinsic nature of the relata. Accordingly, if the relation of selection is external, whether or not the actual world selects a particular element does not depend upon the intrinsic nature of the element. The realist is thus free to say that the elements are all featureless points. Under this hypothesis, quiet moderate realism is indeed more qualitatively parsimonious than extreme realism, for his elements are all the duplicates of each other.

Lewis has two objections to the hypothesis that the relation of selection is external: as before, the quiet moderate realist cannot understand his own primitive; and there are magical necessary connections between elements and the world.

I cannot see why the moderate realist's grasp of "selects" should still be mysterious. Lewis writes "so far as we are told, selection is not any external relation which is ever instantiated entirely within the concrete world ... I wonder how such a relation even can come within the reach of our thought and language."[25] Now, the problem of understanding articulated in the previous section relied upon the assumption that the relation was internal. To grasp an internal relation, it seemed, one had to have a conception of the intrinsic properties on which that relation supervened. Without this, I can find no analogous argument.

Indeed, an argument that showed that we could not have words for an external relation that was never instantiated entirely within the concrete world would have deep and troubling consequences: the intelligibility of set theory itself would be threatened, as the relation *is a member of* is just such a relation.[26] This is seen as follows. Suppose *a* and *b* are perfect duplicates. Despite the fact that they share all their intrinsic properties, *a* is a member of {*a*} while *b* is not; so whether or not an object is a member of a set does not supervene upon the intrinsic nature of the relata, and hence the relation *is a member of* is external. However, just like *selects*, the relation *is a member of* is not instantiated entirely within the concrete world. So if a relation must, in some instance, be instantiated by a pair of objects, both of which are part of the concrete world, to be intelligible, then set theory is unintelligible. This conclusion is hard to accept. Not only is set theory a central discipline in mathematics, but philosophy abounds with set-theoretic constructions. Model theory for modal and predicate languages alike uses set-theoretic constructions (and Lewis himself identifies properties and propositions with set-theoretic constructions out of possibilia[27] – although this is an area where Lewis's theory has applications outside the modal realm).

Let us turn, then, to Lewis's second charge: that the quiet moderate realist must postulate magical necessary connections. Recall that the necessary connections form part of the quiet moderate realist's minimal view about representation: an element e represents that a donkey talks if, necessarily, when the concrete world contains a talking donkey then, and only then, e is selected by the concrete world. But Lewis complains that, if the relation of selection is external, then this necessary connection is mysterious. He writes:

> What makes a relation external, I would have thought, exactly is that it holds independently of the natures of the two *relata*. We wanted the relation to be independent of the intrinsic natures of the elements ... But now we want the relation not to be independent of what goes on within the concrete world. How can we have it both ways?[28]

The objection seems to be that the behaviour of the selection relation required by the quiet moderate realist contradicts the fact that it is an *external* relation. Given the concrete world w, and given the abstract element e, *a donkey talks*, if we are told that the concrete world contains a talking donkey then it *follows* that w selects e. But if selection is an external relation it seems as if this could not be right: an external relation is supposed to hold independently of the intrinsic natures of the relata.

But this appearance of tension is in fact illusory. An external relation holds independently of the intrinsic *natures* of the relata. This means that, given an external relation R, and objects a and b, it should be possible for there to be objects x and y *just like a and b* that are related by R, and also possible for there to be objects x' and y' also *just like a and b* that are not related by R. *The quiet moderate realist's position is entirely compatible with this.* As mentioned above, if selection is external then the quiet moderate realist can take all the elements to be featureless points. If he does this, then all the elements (trivially) have the same intrinsic natures. Suppose that the actual concrete world w^*, containing as it does a talking philosopher, selects the element *e*, *there is a talking philosopher*. The very same world, *w**, does not select the element *d*, *there is a talking donkey*. Trivially, *w** and *w** have the same nature. Moreover, since *e* and *d* are both featureless points, they too share the same intrinsic properties. However, *w** bears the selection relation to *d*, while *w** does not bear the selection relation to *e*. This implies that the relation of selection is external.

It is true that there is a necessary connection between the world's containing a talking donkey, and the particular element *there is a talking donkey* being selected. But this necessary connection is not forbidden by the definition of "external", for there is no implication from this necessary connection that, magically, the selection relation supervenes upon the intrinsic natures of the concrete world and of the element *there is a talking donkey*. In fact, the intrinsic nature of the element is entirely irrelevant here. The reason the relation of selection holds in this case is not because of the intrinsic properties of *d* but because of the *identity* of the element: it is the fact that the element is the very entity *there is a talking donkey* that implies it is selected if the world contains a talking donkey. Whether or not a relation is external depends only on the natures of the relata, and *not* the relata's identity. So the necessary connection currently between the world's containing a talking donkey and the particular element *there is a talking donkey* being selected is compatible with the selection relation being external. Thus, if we wish to show that the necessary connections are problematic, we need assumptions that go beyond the mere externality of the selection relation.

The situation is illustrated by considering the *distance* relation. *Distance* is a paradigm external relation. Whether or not *a* is five metres away from *b* is independent of the intrinsic natures of *a* and *b*. However, this is quite compatible with the view that it is *necessary* that space-time point *a* be five metres away from space-time point *b*. The fact that these two things are five metres apart does not follow from their natures – there are duplicates of *a* and *b* that are six metres apart. But given that it is *this* space-time point and *that* space-time point that have been chosen, one may accept that it is necessary that *they* be five metres apart without contradicting the view that *distance* is external. We might say that the fact that a relation is external tells us something about what *qualitative* possibilities there are (that R is external implies that there are duplicates of a and b that do stand in the relation R, and other duplicates of a and b that do not) but that this does not conflict with a view about what is impossible or otherwise for certain *individuals* (thus it may be still be necessary that *a itself* and *b itself* stand in the R relation).

As a matter of fact, the externality of the relation is *not* the only assumption that Lewis appeals to in his argument. Elsewhere, Lewis claims that the kind of necessary connections postulated by the realist are in tension with a particular extension of his principle of *recombination*. Recall that this is the principle we saw the extreme realist use to try to guarantee that there were all the possible worlds there ought to be: that there were no gaps in logical space.[29] Roughly, this principle denies that there are any necessary connections between distinct existences. But this is spelled out by Lewis in terms of *duplicates*. For instance, it follows from the principle that, if it is possible for Fred and his father Harry to exist, then it is possible for a duplicate of Fred to exist alone. Note that the conclusion is that it is possible for a *duplicate* of Fred to exist alone, and not that it is possible for *Fred* to exist alone, for we might not count anything as Fred in any scenario where his father did not exist. Perhaps it is one of Fred's individuating conditions that he is the son of his father.

At first sight, this may appear to be something of a surprise. One would have thought that the denial of necessary connections between distinct existences would be incompatible with the view that, necessarily, where Fred exists Harry exists. However, the Humean principle essentially derives from the idea that all necessary connections should have their source in relations between concepts or ideas or, in more modern terms, that all necessary connections should really be grounded in semantics. Since, for Lewis, we may just not count anything as a counterpart of Fred unless he is the son of a counterpart of Harry, the necessary connection is explained in terms of a linguistic connection. As such, even Hume himself should find such a necessary connection wholly unmysterious.

Lewis objects that it *is* mysterious how, given that the world contains a talking donkey, it is *necessary* that the world selects the element *a donkey talks* rather than the element *a donkey walks*:

> It seems to be one fact that somewhere within the concrete world, a donkey talks; and an entirely independent fact that the

concrete world enters into an external relation with this element and not with that. What stops it going the other way?[30]

As he admits, the principle of recombination as it has already been articulated does not, on its own, rule out such necessary connections, for the principle rules out only necessary connections between *distinct* existences and, in this case, the concrete world that contains a talking donkey is the *same* as the concrete world that selects a particular element. Nevertheless, Lewis thinks it entirely natural to extend this principle so that it equally rules out necessary connections between the intrinsic character of a thing and the external relations it bears to other things.

Unfortunately, Lewis doesn't tell us how to formalize his extended principle of recombination. In particular, I would like to know which of the following two principles he takes to be entailed by the extended principle:

(1) Let R be an external relation; if it is possible that a bears/does not bear R to b while a has intrinsic property F, then it is equally possible that a does not bear/bears R to b while a has intrinsic property F.

(2) Let R be an external relation; if it is possible that a bears/does not bear R to b while a has intrinsic property F, then it is equally possible that there is a duplicate of a and a duplicate of b and a does not bear/bears R to b.

Remember that, for Lewis, the original principle of recombination is understood in terms of *duplicates*. Given a world according to which there is an F, and given a world according to which there is a G, there is a world according to which there is a duplicate of the F and a duplicate of the G. Accordingly, by analogy, we might expect the extension of this principle to be formulated in terms of duplicates, and so take (2) to be the correct version. But, unfortunately for Lewis, (2) poses no more of a threat for the quiet moderate realist than the fact that *selection* is an external relation. Since selected elements, such as *a donkey walks*, are duplicates of unselected elements, such as *a donkey talks*, then we find the actual world bearing/not bearing R to an object a while a duplicate of the actual world (namely the actual world again) bears/doesn't bear *R* to a duplicate of *a*. If the extended principle of recombination is formulated in terms of duplicates, then the quiet moderate realist has nothing to fear from it.

By contrast, the quiet moderate realist could not accept (1). If the concrete world contains a talking donkey then, necessarily, the element *a donkey talks* is selected. Unfortunately for Lewis, it's not clear that *he* can accept (1) either. The same reasons that prompted Lewis to formulate his original principle of recombination in terms of duplicates apply here. Lewis allows that it is necessary that, where Harry exists, his father exists, because nothing deserves the name "Harry" unless it is the son of Fred. Similarly, I can see no reason to rule out names for which there are semantic conventions dictating that nothing deserves the name *a* unless it bears an external relation *R* to an *F*-thing. Perhaps the quiet moderate realist will say that names for his abstract elements have precisely this quality.

Indeed, if we formulate the extension of the principle of recombination using names rather than duplicates, then we run the risk of generating distinct worlds that are inimical to Lewis's realism. Let us look again at the last quote from Lewis:

> It seems to be one fact that somewhere within the concrete world, a donkey talks; and an entirely independent fact that the concrete world enters into a certain external relation with this element and not with that. What stops it from going the other way?

It sounds as if Lewis thinks there should be two different possibilities here: one where the concrete world selects *a* and not *b*, and another possibility where the concrete world, just as it actually is, selects *b* and not *a*. *But this gives rise to possibilities that are qualitatively indiscernible*. Let us suppose that there are infinitely many elements that the concrete world selects and infinitely many elements that the concrete world fails to select. As before, call the element *a donkey talks d* and the element *a philosopher walks e*. Then Lewis is here asking us to contrast the possibility where the concrete world selects infinitely many elements, including *d*, and fails to select infinitely many elements, including *e*, with a different possibility where the concrete world, just as it was, selects infinitely many elements, including *e*, and fails to select infinitely many elements, including *d*. However, since *e* and *d* are duplicates of each other, we see that there is no qualitative difference between these two possibilities. But the contentious view that there are distinct possibilities that are qualitatively identical should *not* be a consequence of the principle of recombination. Lewis himself explicitly rejects this view and, besides, what began as an innocuous enough principle – the Humean denial of necessary connections between distinct existences – has now metamorphosed into a highly contentious doctrine.

There is a final twist in the tail, for there *is* a combinatorialist principle that the quiet moderate realist violates, which is suggested by Lewis's argument. We might extend the combinatorialist principle by insisting that any *pattern* of elements selected by the concrete world ought to be compatible with any intrinsic features of the concrete world. Thus, if selection is an external relation, it ought to be possible for the concrete world to contain a talking donkey and for it to select *every single element*. Equally, it ought to be possible for the concrete world to contain a talking donkey, and for it to bear the selection relation to *no* elements at all. After all, one might argue (in a Lewisian spirit), it seems to be one fact that the concrete world contains a talking donkey, and another, quite separate, fact that the world bears the selection relation to any element at all. And note here that, this time, the possibilities that we are being asked to distinguish *are* genuinely qualitatively different. This version of the principle of recombination could not be tolerated by the quiet moderate realist.

Unfortunately for Lewis, this version cannot be tolerated by him either. Applying this verion to the *is a member* relation, it follows that there are genuine possible worlds containing things that do not bear the *is a member of* relation to *any* set; similarly, there are possible worlds containing two distinct sets that have exactly the same members. Neither of these consequences is palatable. If there are possible individuals that are not members of any set, then it seems as if Lewis can no longer identify the property *F* with the set of all objects that are *F*, for if one of the possible *F*-things is not a member of any set, then there is no set containing all and only the *F*-things. Yet it is precisely this set that Lewis needs in his construction. Similarly, Lewis will have problems justifying the use of possible world model theory as there is no longer a set containing all possible objects. And the conclusion that there could be two sets that had exactly the same members seems even worse, for many think it part of the concept of a set that only one set can have *these* very members. The members that a set has are thought of as being constitutive of that set's identity. This thesis has modal implications: it's not just that, as a matter of fact, one set *does* have these very members, but that only one set *could* have these very members.

Lewis's argument against the quiet moderate realist has foundered. The principles that tell against the quiet moderate realist are principles that Lewis himself does not even hold, and the principles that Lewis does find plausible turn out not to be violated by the quiet moderate realist.

Conclusion

Lewis's attempted knock-down argument against quiet moderate realism fails. However, quiet moderate realism has some way to go to deliver on its initial promise. Neither the view that worlds are sets of propositions nor the view that they are maximal states of affairs delivers a particularly attractive or safe and sane ontology; indeed, it is not even clear whether the world-making elements deserve to be called states of affairs at all. Nor is the ideology particularly attractive. It is downright peculiar to take "is true at" as a primitive of the theory (and don't be fooled if the quiet moderate realist uses an apparently familiar word such as *obtains, instantiates* or *holds* for the same primitive – whatever the name, it's still a bizarre primitive) and we are told so little about this primitive that we may feel unsure whether we have been given a theory at all. Moreover, the quiet moderate realist seems committed to further primitives if he is going to get possible worlds to do useful work, such as a primitive notion of *closeness* to analyse counterfactuals. Worse, neither the view that worlds are sets of propositions nor the view that they are recombinations of elements of the actual world manages to generate a set of things capable of playing the role of possibilia. Without such a set, the applications of possible worlds theory are limited; it is not clear how to justify the use of possible worlds semantics, nor is it clear how to translate sentences comparing the domains of different worlds or modalized comparatives. Plantinga's individual essences may help the quiet moderate realist to some of these applications, but accepting such things as individual essences of nonexistent entities is a difficult step to take.

Possible worlds as sets
7 of sentences

In this chapter we examine the view that possible worlds are essentially sets of sentences. We call this position the *linguistic theory*. Unlike the quiet moderate realist, the linguistic theorist has something to say about representation, about what it is for a proposition to be true at a world. Propositions are true at worlds in much the same way as they are true at books: by being implied by the book. Indeed, linguistic theorists may even *define* the phrase "true at w". In this way, the linguistic theorist hopes to avoid the unnatural and magical primitives of the quiet moderate realist. The main problem facing the linguistic theorist is generating enough books to represent all the possibilities that we pre-theoretically wish to accept. The linguistic theorist will need a rich and flexible world-making language if he is to have any hope of doing this.

Accepting a linguistic theory may not be the only way to generate a moderate ontology containing possible worlds without taking "true at w" as a primitive. One might develop the idea that worlds represent in the same way that a map represents; namely, by sharing some kind of structure with that which is represented. Unfortunately, this idea quickly leads to trouble: a map represents by sharing similar properties to the land it represents. We need possible worlds according to which there are talking donkeys and if the worlds do this by containing something that shares similar properties to a talking donkey then the position begins to look like nothing more than extreme realism.[1]

The view that possible worlds should be identified with sets of sentences has a long and distinguished history: Carnap identified worlds with sets that, for every atomic sentence of some interpreted language, contain either that sentence or its negation;[2] Jeffrey suggested that possible worlds should be identified with complete, consistent novels;[3] and Hintikka argued that possible worlds should be taken to be maximally consistent sets of sentences.[4] But does the linguistic theory deserve to be called a *realism* about possible worlds? After all, if there weren't any language users there wouldn't be any languages, and without any languages there wouldn't be any books. Accordingly, if worlds are nothing more than books then it would seem as if the existence of worlds themselves depends upon facts about language users and so we appear to have an *anti*-realist view of worlds. The linguistic theorist has a realist response available: he need not take books to be anything like the pen and paper affairs that we are used to. Rather, books can be identified with set-theoretic constructions of particulars and universals – these things *would* exist whether or not there are language users.

The critic may still doubt that we have a form of realism here, for he may urge that, even if the books themselves can be identified with objects whose existence owes nothing to us, a mere string of symbols cannot, in and of itself, represent that *P* is the case. Rather, the representational properties of such strings derive from facts about the thought and behaviour of the community that uses that string of symbols. Without language users, strings of symbols just wouldn't represent anything. The *worlds* themselves may exist independently of language users, but what is the case according to these worlds surely does not. Again, the critic concludes, such a position does not seem to deserve to be called a realism about possible worlds.

This point is well made. And it may be that many who accept the linguistic theory should not be classed as realists about possible worlds. But one arguably *should* be a realist if the possible worlds framework is more than a mere heuristic and is used to do serious philosophical work. Fortunately, linguistic theorists who wish to remain realists again have a defence, for they can argue that the world-making language of the linguistic theorist is not one that we need to speak or write down; the world-making language can be far removed from the kinds of languages people use. For modal purposes all that is required is that, for all possible *P*, there are many entities *w* such that *P* is *true at w*, and that the words "true at" are *not* taken as a primitive (which would lead to a quiet moderate realism) but are adequately defined. The linguistic theorist's worlds will have to have a certain amount of structure for such a definition to succeed – and it is essentially nothing more than the need for such structure that gives this theory the name "linguistic"[5] – but although this structure gives the linguistic theorist the chance to define the words "true at", the *relation* that these words pick out is itself an objective feature of reality. Given the linguistic theorist's definition of "true at", the fact that donkeys talk is true at *w* is a fact that holds entirely independently of the existence or conventions of language users. In this way, the linguistic theorist can regain his right to be called a *realist*.

What should the linguistic theorist take the sentences of his world-making language to be? As usual, there should be enough sentences to represent *all* the possible ways the world could be, or the resultant theory will fail to recapture the equivalence between *P*'s being possible and the existence of a world at which *P* is true. As a start, it would be nice to have names for every object and predicates for every property or, at least, a set of predicates rich enough to express every property. Is this a tall order? Not at all. Such a language is readily available: accept the Lagadonian solution and let each particular name itself and each property or relation be its own predicate. Simply let the atomic sentences be *n*-tuples of the form $<R, a, \ldots, b>$ where R is an $(n - 1)$-place relation (or property) and $a, \ldots, b$ are $n - 1$ particulars. Interpret any such *n*-tuple as saying that the entities $a, \ldots, b$, in that order, stand in the relation R. Possible worlds might now be identified with the *maximally consistent* atomic sentences.[6]

So developed, the linguistic theory is like the version of combinatorialism discussed previously. It promises to provide a reasonably safe and sane ontology: all it postulates are actually existing particulars, actually instantiated properties and set-theoretic constructions thereof. Still, it is scarcely ontologically innocent: sets must be accepted into our ontology and properties must also be reified. So, as it stands, the linguistic theory is not acceptable to the nominalist. Unlike combinatorialism, the linguistic theorist is not committed to the view that *any* set of ordered *n*-tuples counts as a *possible* world. Thus the combinatorialist's problem of incompatible properties is avoided. Perhaps most importantly, there need be no mystery about how the linguistic theorist's worlds represent. Recombinations are to be understood as *sentences* whose content can be spelled out as follows:

(1) For any particular *a*, and every property *F*, the atomic sentence "*a* has property *F*" is true at *w* iff $<F, a> \in w$
(2) For any particulars *a...b*, and every relation *R*, the atomic sentence "*a*, ..., *b* are related by relation *R*" is true at *w* iff $<R, a, ..., b> \in w$
(3) for *any* non-modal sentence *S*, *S* is true at *w* iff the atomic sentences true at *w* entail *S*.

As a matter of fact, the linguistic theorist can step back from the Lagadonian solution in two respects while not diminishing the representational potential of his world-making language. First, it is not necessary for the linguistic theorist to insist that his world-making language contain names for every single thing. In particular, he does not need names for necessarily existing objects such as numbers and sets, or predicates for their properties. Even if sentences such as "3 < 4" cannot be formulated in his world-making language, they will still be true at his worlds, for, being necessary, such truths will be trivially entailed by any world, and thus by (3) will be true at any world. Later, we shall take advantage of the linguistic theorist's ability to do this.

Secondly, the linguistic theorist does not need a predicate for every actually instantiated property and relation: predicates for all the fundamental properties and relations will suffice. A description at the basic level, which talks only of microscopic processes and the properties and relations that fundamental objects instantiate, nevertheless entails truths about the existence of macroscopic objects such as cabbages and kings. So again, by clause (3), propositions about such things can be true or false at worlds, even if the world-making language lacks predicates for such things. This is metaphysically desirable because it means that the linguistic theorist can buy into an attractive theory of properties, such as Armstrong's theory of universals, or trope theory. Rather than having to accept into his ontology unnatural kinds of properties, such as the property of being a cabbage or the property of being a king, he can describe worlds at which it is true that there are cabbages and kings using predicates for only the most fundamental properties, such as *being charged* or *having mass*: properties that truly do cut nature at the joint, that truly do make for similarity between different particulars.

Indeed, if this route is taken, even nominalists may eventually be able to buy into the linguistic theory, for if it turns out that there are a finite number of fundamental properties and relations, and if we eventually discover what these properties and relations are, then the linguistic theorist can avoid the quantification over properties that appear in clauses (2) and (3) above by replacing them with clauses *using* the relevant predicates. The linguistic theorist will need as many clauses as there are fundamental properties and relations, but if there are only finitely many of these, he will be able to complete his definition of "true at". Of course, this resource is not available to the nominalist right now, as fundamental physics is as yet unfinished, but at some future time those who wish to eschew even properties may accept the linguistic theory.

Although the linguistic theorist offers an account of the "true at" relation and although his ontology and ideology may be attractive, the philosophical applications of the linguistic theory are limited in familiar ways. Like the quiet moderate realists, the linguistic theorist is unable to use his theory of possible worlds to provide non-circular analyses of □ and ◇. Both in defining which sets of atomic sentences were the possible worlds (the maximally *consistent* ones) and in clause (3) above (where the modal notion of *entailment* is used) the theory takes modality as primitive.

Like most quiet moderate realists, most linguistic theorists have not offered us an ontology of *possibilia*. As we have seen, without possibilia it is unclear how a theorist can help himself to the possible worlds translations of "There could have been more things than there actually are", and the like, or how he can formalize modalized comparatives. Again, without possibilia there are problems over how to justify the use of possible worlds semantics for quantificational logic.

However, it may well be possible to use linguistic resources to create an ontology of possibilia. Perhaps, just as, for the linguistic theorist, worlds are complete sets of sentences, possibilia should be taken to be maximal sets of one-place predicates, each predicate describing a complete way a possible object could be.[7]

On such a proposal, we will say that a particular possible object exists at a world precisely when its existential closure exists at that world. Or perhaps possibilia should be taken to be nothing more than names, the constants of the linguistic theorist's world-making language. In this case, we might say that a particular possible object exists at a world precisely if its name appears in one of the atomic sentences there. In either case, detailed philosophical work is needed to see whether such proposals will enable the linguistic theorist to help himself to the full power of the possible worlds framework.

Missing possibilities

Unfortunately, the linguistic theory faces some serious difficulties dealing with modal truth itself. As with combinatorialism, this linguistic theory is unable to accommodate the possibilities that there could have been non-actual particulars and alien properties.[8] The sentences of the linguistic theorist's world-making language only contain names and predicates for actual particulars and predicates for actually instantiated properties; accordingly, his world-making language is unable to describe possible worlds that contain non-actual particulars or where alien properties are instantiated. As we have already urged, the possibility of such worlds is highly plausible[9] and an adequate theory should allow for it.

Fortunately, unlike the combinatorialist, the linguistic theorist has the resources to deal with this difficulty. By including the existential quantifier and the identity symbol in his world-making language, and extending his definition of "true at", he can write down a sentence according to which there are non-actual particulars and alien properties. With these devices to hand, the linguistic theorist can generate a sentence of the form $\exists x(x \neq a \,\&\, x \neq b \,\&\, \ldots \,\&\, x \neq c)$, where $a, b, \ldots, c$ is a list of all the particulars that actually exist.

But hold on. If the linguistic theorist's world-making language is such that every particular is its own name and every property its own predicate, then where in his ontology can he find the extra words for $\exists$ and new variables $x, y, z, \ldots$? We noted earlier that the linguistic theorist didn't actually need names for numbers or pure sets, so these things are not part of his world-making language. He can take advantage of this to use these free elements from the set-theoretic hierarchy as his new words for ∃ and for variables. Clauses (1)–(4) need to be supplemented to allow for worlds containing these new existentially quantified formulas. But the only new resources we have introduced are quite familiar from the predicate calculus, and defining the truth of these new sentences is a relatively straightforward matter.

Since the linguistic theorist is capable of generating worlds according to which there are non-actual particulars and properties, it seems as if he has avoided the worst difficulties that beset the combinatorialist. Unfortunately, this way of representing possibilities containing non-actual objects and alien properties still runs into difficulties. To understand these difficulties, we need to examine the modal doctrine of *haecceitism*.

Haecceitism

Consider a simple world w, containing three objects, a, b and c, such that a and b are F, c is G and nothing else holds at that world. Is there another world, w', distinct from w, that also contains three objects, a, b and c, save that at w', a and c are F, and b is G and nothing else happens?

Suppose that sentence S, a (possibly infinite) conjunction, describes in perfect detail the qualitative character of some possible world. Replacing every occurrence of some name with a free variable, and then deleting each conjunct not containing that variable, results in a conjunction of open formulas that describes a role a particular may occupy. Let us call such roles *first-order roles*. The two worlds w and w' agree on which first-order roles are occupied, and how many times each role is occupied, but they disagree as to *which* particulars occupy these roles.

Let us call the view that there are distinct worlds agreeing upon which first-order roles are occupied but disagreeing over which individuals play which roles "haecceitism" (but beware because the term "haecceitism" has been used to cover a multitude of different positions). Whether there are haecceitistic differences between worlds is a much discussed issue on which philosophical opinion is currently divided: Lewis and Armstrong are both anti-haecceitists, the later Kaplan is a haecceitist, and Skyrms accepts haecceitism for actual entities, but not for merely possible ones.[10]

In my view, it *is* plausible that there be distinct worlds that differ only over which objects play which roles. Imagine a world containing a solitary cylinder balanced on a plane. Suppose that the situation is perfectly symmetric: all parts of the cylinder are made of the same material; each atomic part of the cylinder has the same intrinsic properties as any other; and the object is a *perfect* cylinder. Similarly, the plane on which the cylinder is resting is completely homogeneous: all the points of the plane share the same intrinsic properties. After a certain time t has elapsed, the rod falls over in a random direction. Intuitively, there are many different ways the rod could fall. We might like to spell this out by saying that there are many different worlds where the rod falls in different directions. However, all these worlds are qualitatively indiscernible: they differ only over *which* points of the plane the cylinder ends up falling towards.

We can also wonder whether there are distinct worlds that differ only over which *properties* play which roles. Consider again sentence S. Replacing every occurrence of some *predicate* with a free variable and then deleting each conjunct not containing that variable results in a conjunction of open formulas that expresses a *second-order role*: that is, a role a property may occupy. Are there distinct worlds that agree upon which second-order roles are occupied but disagree as to which properties occupy these roles? Consider w'' which, like w, contains a, b and c, and is such that a and b are G, c is F and nothing else happens at that world. It is clear that the worlds w and w'' agree upon which second-order roles are occupied, but disagree as to which properties occupy these roles.

I shall call the view that there are distinct worlds that agree as to which property roles are occupied, but differ as to which properties play which roles, *second-order haecceitism*. Second-order haecceitism has not been as widely debated as haecceitism itself, but it is a much more popular doctrine. Thus Lewis and Armstrong, who are both anti-haecceitists, subscribe to second-order haecceitism. I, too, find second-order haecceitism a highly plausible doctrine.

Why is second-order haecceitism plausible? One might simply think it plausible that there could be a possible world, distinct from the actual one, at which two properties of quarks have exchanged roles.[11] However, some believe that properties have their nomological roles, or causal powers, essentially. If so, then quark colour *being red* could not behave as the quark colour *being green*, and thus it seems as though two properties could not exchange nomological roles. Let us distinguish between weak nomological essentialism and strong nomological essentialism. In weak nomological essentialism, a property may occupy its nomological role vacuously. For instance, suppose that it is part of F's nomological role that objects that instantiate it should interact with objects that instantiate G in a certain way under certain circumstances C. Then, according to weak nomological essentialism, F may be said to play this role even if there are no objects that instantiate G, or if conditions C never obtain. In the strong sense, if it is part of F's nomological role that it should interact with Gs under certain conditions, then objects that instantiate G must exist and conditions C must obtain for it to play its role. The view that properties have their nomological role or causal powers strongly essentially is highly implausible,[12] for it means that nothing can be F unless something that is G also exists. Yet there are surely some properties figuring in laws, such as *having mass* or *being coloured*, that are *intrinsic* – that is, properties things have in virtue of the way they themselves are – *not* in virtue of their relations to other things. But if an object cannot be an F without a G existing, F cannot be an intrinsic property.

Nomological essentialism is therefore much more plausible in its weak form. Now, it is possible to describe two possible worlds that differ only over which properties play which roles, and at each world the properties instantiated occupy their nomological roles vacuously. Consider two rather simple worlds w and w' such that both contain only object a, but a instantiates different properties at the two worlds. The second-order role occupied at these two worlds is expressed by the formula Xa. Thus at both w and w', precisely the same second-order role is occupied: being instantiated by a. Yet a world containing one particle that instantiates the property *being charged* is surely different from a world containing a particle that instantiates the property *having mass*. Accordingly, second-order haecceitism stands and there are distinct worlds that differ only over which properties occupy which roles.

Unfortunately, as Lewis and Bricker have pointed out,[13] the linguistic theory currently under consideration conflates these distinct possibilities, for a scheme that uses existential sentences to generate worlds containing alien properties is unable to generate worlds that differ only over which alien properties occupy which roles. The sentences that represent worlds with alien properties say only that there are so-and-so roles that are occupied by alien properties; they do not say which properties occupy these roles.

The difficulty facing the linguistic theorist is best illustrated by an example. Consider two simple worlds v and v'. At v, a and b are green, while c is red and at v', a and b are red while c is green. These two worlds differ only over which properties play which roles, but since v contains two green things and one red thing, while v' contains two red things and one green thing, they are clearly distinct. Now consider two worlds V and V'. V is like v above, save that the properties *being red* and *being green* are replaced by two distinct alien properties. V' stands to V as v' stands to v: the property that a and b instantiate at V is instantiated by c at V', and the property that c instantiates at V is instantiated by a and b at V'. Again, since V contains two things instantiating some alien property X and one thing instantiating some other alien property Y, while V' contains two things instantiating Y and one thing instantiating X, the two worlds are distinct.

Lacking predicates for alien properties, the linguistic theorist represents world V with the following sentence:

[*] $\exists X \exists Y (X \neq F \ \& \ X \neq G \ \& \ ... \ \& \ Y \neq F \ \& \ Y \neq G \ \& \ ...$
       $\& \ X \neq Y \ \& \ Xa \ \& \ Xb \ \& \ Yc)$

Unfortunately, this sentence also represents V', for V' is just like W in that there are two alien properties at V' such that a and b instantiate one of these properties and c instantiates the other. So if possible worlds *were* identified with sentences, both V and V' would be identified with the same sentence, [*] above, and so the distinct worlds V and V' would be conflated.

Of course, V and V' are distinct only if second-order haecceitism would be true of alien properties as well as actually instantiated ones. One might argue that second-order haecceitism is false of *alien* properties because our conception of alien properties is different from our conception of actual ones.[14] The argument here is that, since we think of alien properties as merely *analogous* to actual ones, we do not think of haecceitism as being true of them. But it is not at all clear why the fact that we think of alien properties as analogous to actual entities means that haecceitism should fail for alien properties. Indeed, quite the opposite conclusion follows: if merely possible properties are analogous to actual ones, and haecceitism is true of actually instantiated properties, then haecceitism should be true of merely possible properties as well.

A solution

We have seen that identifying possible worlds with existential sentences conflates distinct possibilities. But *must* the linguistic theorist conflate distinct possibilities? Both Lewis and Bricker seem to think that he must because the linguistic theorist can never have names and predicates for all the non-actual particulars and alien properties, and so can never say which particulars and properties play which roles. But while the having of names and predicates may be *sufficient* for distinguishing the possible worlds in question, it is not *necessary* for distinguishing these worlds.

Consider again the worlds V and V', which the theory conflated. What distinguishes V from V'? I maintain it is the following facts: (i) the property that a and b instantiate at V is not *identical* to the property that a and b instantiate at V', but is *identical* to the property that c instantiates at V'; and (ii) the property that c instantiates at V is not *identical* to the property that c instantiates at V', but is *identical* to the property that a and b instantiate at V. Yet these two facts involve merely the transworld identity or non-identity of properties. In order to distinguish V from V', the linguistic theorist does not have to say which properties play which roles; all he needs to say is which properties playing which roles at V are identical or distinct from which properties playing which roles at V'.

What is true of this particular example is true in general. Haecceitism and second-order haecceitism are the views that there are distinct possible worlds that differ only over which particulars or properties play which roles. Or, equivalently, that there are distinct worlds w and w' such that the same roles are occupied at w and w', but some particular/property playing role r at w is not *identical* to some particular/property playing role r at w', and may be *identical* to some particular/property playing role r' at w'. Thus to distinguish two possible worlds differing only over which roles are occupied, the realist merely needs a way of representing the transworld identity of alien entities; he does *not* have to say which alien entities occupy which roles and accordingly does not need names and predicates for them.

To represent transworld identity, the world-making language must be enriched. This can be done in the following way. Just as the identity of actually existing atomic entities across worlds was represented by the same particular entity (that entity's name or predicate) appearing in different sets of sentences, so shall the identity of alien entities across worlds be represented. Whereas before we used actually existing particulars and actually instantiated properties as their own names and predicates, non-actual particulars and alien properties are not part of our ontology, so we must use some other range of objects to represent them and their transworld identity. Just as the same name appearing in the sentences Fa and Ga represents that the same particular satisfies F and G, so the same pseudo-name appearing in the sentences Fc_j and Gc_j represents that the same particular satisfies F and G.

However, pseudo-names are not names and pseudo-predicates are not predicates. Fc_j cannot be understood in precisely the same way as Fa, for c_j, unlike a, does not denote anything. Thus, to interpret worlds containing the sentence, we must treat Fc_j as an existential formula: it is true iff there is some object that is F. Now consider the two sets of sentences $\{Fc_j, Hc_j\}$ and $\{Fc_j, Gc_j\}$. The first set says that there is an object that is F and there is an object that is H. But since the same pseudo-name appears in both sentences, and since we are operating under the convention that sameness of pseudo-name represents sameness of entity, the first set also represents that the thing that is F is also H. Moreover, since the second set contains sentences in which the pseudo-name c_j appears, the second set represents the same object that was F and H according to the first set as being F and G. In this way the transworld identity of non-actual particulars can be represented. Similarly, another set of pseudo-predicates C_j can represent the transworld identity of alien properties.

To implement this idea it is necessary to supplement our world-making language with a set of pseudo-names c_a and pseudo-predicates C_j. Again, we can do this by helping ourselves to elements from the mathematical hierarchy. Syntactically, pseudo-names and pseudo-predicates behave just like ordinary names and predicates. Thus, for example, we say that there are some sentences of our world-making language that are of the form $<C_j, a, \ldots, b>$, that every sentence contains at most one pseudo-predicate and that if a sentence contains a pseudo-predicate, then the pseudo-predicate appears in the first place of that sentence. Similarly, it is important to ensure that the adicity of the alien property that a pseudo-predicate represents remains constant, and so we say that if there is an n-tuple of our world-making language that is a sentence containing C_j, then every sentence that contains C_j is an n-tuple.

We now need to give the interpretations of sentences that contain pseudo-names and pseudo-predicates. We give clauses for the pseudo-predicates – the pseudo-names are similar.

(1) For any two sentences $<C_j, a, \ldots, b>$ and $<C_j, a', \ldots, b'>$, if the first is a member of w and the second is a member of w' (where w' and w may be identical) then it is true at w that there is some alien property X that relates $a, \ldots, b$ at w, and some alien property Y at w' which relates $a', \ldots, b'$ at w', and $X = Y$.

(2) For any two sentences $<C_j, a, \ldots, b>$ and $<C_k, a', \ldots, b'>$ $(j \neq k)$, if the first is a member of w and the second a member of w', then it is true at w that there is some alien property X that relates $a, \ldots, b$ at w, and some alien universal Y at w' that relates $a', \ldots, b'$ at w', and $X \neq Y$.

It should be clear how we can represent worlds that differ only over which alien properties play which roles. Consider the sentences $[d \ \& \ \varphi(C_j) \ \& \ \psi(C_k)]$ (which we'll call world w) and $[d \ \& \ \varphi(C_k) \ \& \ \psi(C_j)]$ (which we'll call w'), where d contains no occurrences of pseudo-predicates. Each of the sentences will be true on its own iff d is true and if there are alien properties that instantiate roles φ and ψ. However, because the two pseudo-predicates occupy different roles in these sentences, and because of our interpretation of these pseudo-predicates, it is also true that, at w, the alien property that plays role φ there plays role ψ at the second, and vice versa. Thus the two distinct possibilities are duly acknowledged, and are not conflated by this version of the linguistic theory.

This version of the linguistic theory also meets Lewis's complaint that there are many ways in which a sentence of the form $\exists X[d \ \& \ \varphi(X)]$ could come true, because, for every pseudo-predicate C_j, there is a sentence $[d \ \& \ \varphi(c_j)]$. Each of these sentences is true iff *d* is true, and if there is an alien property that occupies role φ, but each such sentence represents a different possible world because different properties are represented at different worlds.

Although we may have found ways of getting around two particular sentences that are problematic for the linguistic theorist, it may be wondered why we should be confident that no more of a similar kind may be found. The reply is that the reason that the sentences are problematic stems from the fact that we cannot name alien properties, combined with the fact that haecceitism is true of alien properties (as it is true of actual properties). Since we could name actual properties we could represent the identity of properties across worlds by using the same predicate in different worlds. As Lewis and Bricker correctly argued, speaking of alien properties by quantification did not enable us to represent identity of properties across worlds. But identity of properties across worlds *can* be represented when the world-making language is enriched in the way that has been suggested.

Objections

Lewis has raised an objection against a relation of the above proposal. As mentioned above, Lewis complained that although the existential sentence $\exists X \exists Y[d \ \& \ \varphi(X) \ \& \ \psi(Y)]$ could come true in many ways, since there is only one existential sentence for each of the many ways in which the existential sentence could come true, over what is the expression "there are many ways" quantifying? Lewis considers the reply that we should take ordered pairs of the existential sentence and the natural numbers, thus getting many representations of the possibility that $\exists X \exists Y[d \ \& \ \varphi(X) \ \& \ \psi(Y)]$ represents, over which the quantifier "there are many" may range. He complains that although we may now have multiplicity, this multiplicity is not what he wanted:

> we have the infinitely many new representations, differing by the integers built into them; and we have the infinitely many possibilities, differing by the permutations of the alien properties, that ought to be acknowledged. But the many representations do not represent the many possibilities unambiguously, one to one.[15]

I agree with Lewis that the proposal is flawed, but not for Lewis's reason. Lewis claims that the linguistic theorist's worlds are ambiguous, but this is not true. Something is ambiguous if it has more than one meaning, such as the word "bank". But the existential sentences that Lewis considers are formulated in a well-defined language, and possess a determinate meaning. I grant that a particular existential sentence does not fully represent one of Lewis's possible worlds, but this is not to say it is ambiguous. The sentence "Socrates is snub-nosed" does not fully represent a possible world, but this does not make it ambiguous.

My difficulty with the proposal Lewis considers is that I cannot see how, in the suggested construction, different ways in which the existential sentence could come true are represented. Nor do I see how the construction manages to generate possible worlds where an alien entity that plays role φ at one world plays role ψ at another, for each representation says exactly the same thing. Pairing each representation with a number merely results in a set of sentences that all say the same thing. This is not so on my theory. By the construction above, the alien property that plays the role φ at the world $[d \& \varphi(C_j) \& \psi(C_k)]$ plays the role ψ at the world $[d \& \varphi(C_k) \& \psi(C_j)]$. Moreover, the two worlds $[d \& \varphi(C_k)]$ and $[d \& \varphi(C_j)]$ represent different ways in which the sentence $\exists X[d \& \varphi(X)]$ could be true, because the alien properties that are instantiated according to the two sentences are different.

Lewis might argue against this proposal. He might say that pseudo-predicate C_k does not represent one particular alien property, but is ambiguous over all the possible alien properties. Thus each such world that contains a pseudo-predicate for an alien property represents not only a possible world, but ambiguously represents many. And so, Lewis might conclude, nothing has been gained.

Again the linguistic theorist can object to the charge that his worlds are ambiguous. It is true that pseudo-predicates do not represent one alien property rather than another, but this does not make them ambiguous. A set of sentences containing a pseudo-predicate that is true at w and true at w', neither represents w nor w'. This is not to say that this set of sentences represents ambiguously. The set quite determinately says, among other things, that there is an alien property that does such and such.

Nevertheless, it must be granted that there is some slack. A set of sentences that contains a pseudo-predicate only represents an incomplete possible world, or a *possibility*, for it does not tell us which alien properties occupy which roles. Is this a serious problem?

I think not, for I agree with Stalnaker that there is no reason to believe why possible worlds *should* be complete:

> nothing in the formalism of possible worlds semantics, or in the intuitive conception of a way things might be, or a possible state of the world, excludes an interpretation in which possible worlds are alternative states of some limited subject matter.[16]

In a similar vein, Hintikka says, "possible worlds semantics was always intended, by myself at least, [to be] applied in such a way that the alternatives considered as 'small worlds', as alternative courses an experiment might take", and he laments that "if I had been really smart, I would have called the whole thing 'possible situation semantics'".[17]

The project was to construct worlds that could represent the identity of alien entities across worlds, and I do not see why the fact that each world that contains a pseudo-predicate is incomplete means that they fail to represent whether or not the alien entity that exists according to one such world is identical to or different from the alien entity that exists according to another such world.

Consider an analogy. Suppose that a museum contained a number of paintings by an abstract artist. Some of the paintings are of exactly the same form, differing only over which segments are filled by which particular colour. A number of paintings by Rothko would satisfy this description. Now suppose that the museum prints a catalogue of these paintings. Unfortunately, something goes wrong with the printing and the pictures in the catalogue are not coloured, but are various shades of grey. Despite this error, the catalogue is of high quality, and each particular colour always comes out the same shade of grey and no two different colours ever come out the same shade of grey. Accordingly, a key is provided with the catalogue that says that each shade of grey stands for some particular colour, and that no two shades of grey stand for the same colour. Since the key does not tell us which shade of grey stands for which colour, this catalogue is not a perfect representation of the paintings in the gallery. Nevertheless, it does carry *some* information about these paintings. In particular, it represents the shape of each painting, and represents which regions of each painting are painted the same or different colours. It also represents when the parts of two different paintings are of the same colour, by having the same particular shade of grey occupy different regions on different paintings.

Now consider two of the paintings of precisely the same form: a rectangle divided by a straight horizontal line two-thirds down from the top, say. In one, "Sunrise", the greater area is red and the lesser area is blue, and in the other, "Sunrise in Australia", the greater area is blue and the lesser area is red. Accordingly, there will be two representations of these paintings. Consider one of them. Considered alone, it determinately represents neither "Sunrise" nor "Sunrise in Australia", for there is no key to tell us which shade of grey represents which colour. All it tells us is that there is some painting in the gallery, the upper two-thirds of which is one colour, and the lower third of which is some other colour. Similarly, the other representation, when considered alone, does not determinately represent either picture, and would seem to represent nothing more than the first one.

But although the two in isolation seem to say nothing more than each other, the two taken together say more. Because the shade of grey that fills the greater portion in one is the same shade as that which fills the lesser portion in the other, the two paintings together show that there are two distinct paintings in the gallery, both of the same proportion, but whose colours are permuted. It is still correct to say that each of the representations is ambiguous – neither determinately represents "Sunrise" – but it does not follow that "nothing has been gained". That there are two different paintings is indeed represented by the catalogue.

The same point applies to the linguistic theorist's books. Lewis may complain that for each world that contains a pseudo-predicate the linguistic theorist has not and cannot say which of Lewis's possible worlds this represents. The linguistic theorist must grant this, so makes a significant departure from many realists' aims, for many realists believe that, for every concrete possible world that Lewis believes in, there is a world that determinately represents the facts that obtain in that world. But sentences that contain pseudo-predicates do not determinately represent Lewis's possible worlds. However, it is questionable whether we need such detailed worlds in order to have worlds that represent all the facts of modality. Because our conception of alien entities is merely analogical, our conception of possible worlds is not so fine-grained that we need to say which alien entity each pseudo-predicate stands for. It is enough that my worlds represent the transworld identity of these alien entities.

One might object that there is a significant disanalogy between my worlds and the paintings in the catalogue, for it is a fact, unbeknown to us, which shade of grey in the catalogue represents which colour, as there is a causal connection between the two that determines the colour a particular shade of grey represents. This is not true of the linguistic theorist's pseudo-predicates.

It is true that we *could* have interpreted the pictures in the catalogue in this way and, had we done so, the two cases would indeed have been disanalogous. But we don't have to interpret the pictures in this way, and the key presented above does not do so. That the pictures in the catalogue *could* have been used to represent the paintings determinately is thus irrelevant to the point that, as interpreted by the key, the catalogue and the worlds are perfectly analogous. It seems then that the possible worlds developed in this section are able to represent the transworld identity of alien entities, and are thus able to meet this particular problem.

Conclusion

In my view, the linguistic approach towards possible worlds is a promising research programme. Unlike extreme realism, its ontology is relatively safe and sane. Unlike quiet moderate realism, its ideology is relatively attractive; there are no suspicious primitives of the theory. Moreover, the linguistic theorist has the resources available to him to avoid the charges that he cannot distinguish enough distinct possibilities. But the reason I view it as a promising research programme rather than a fully fledged theory of modality is because questions remain over the linguistic theorist's ability to provide a domain of entities that can be plausibly identified with possibilia as well as possible worlds. Further work then has to be done to see whether the linguistic theorist's postulated possibilia are capable of doing the serious philosophical work the extreme realist's possibilia can do in a reasonably attractive and unproblematic way.

Notes

Chapter 1: Introduction to modality

1. This appears to have been Quine's attitude towards the modal.

2. Quine does indeed offer reasons for thinking that our modal concepts are incoherent. See Chapter 3 for further discussion.

3. This is not to say that this work cannot be done. There are a number of subtle and sophisticated theories that attempt to recover the distinction between a law and a mere accidental regularity without appealing to the modal. But it is still a contentious matter whether any of these theories is successful. For a thorough discussion, see D. M. Armstrong, *What is a Law of Nature?* (Cambridge: Cambridge University Press, 1983).

4. E. Mendelson, *Introduction to Mathematical Logic*, 3rd edn (Monterey, CA: Wadsworth & Brooks/Cole, 1987), 52.

5. Of course, this is not to say that our notion of modality cannot ever be eliminated in favour of some model-theoretic notion. Indeed, later we shall see that certain theorists take possible worlds to be something like the logician's models. At present, my only concern is to defend the modal as a legitimate topic of study by pointing to the central role it plays in various important bodies of knowledge. If one adopts scepticism to the modal in general, as Quine does, then one needs to explain why logic is anything other than an abstract game. For more on this topic see J. Etchemendy, *The Concept of Logical Consequence* (Cambridge, MA: Harvard University Press, 1990).

6. In particular, it is hard to make sense of propositions that seem determined by the axioms, but not provable from the axioms. For instance, second-order set theory determines the truth of the continuum hypothesis, but the continuum hypothesis itself is neither provable nor refutable from the axioms. See G. Hellman, *Mathematics Without Numbers* (Oxford: Clarendon Press, 1989) for a recent and thorough version of "if-then-ism" in mathematics, a version that is thoroughly and unashamedly modal.

7. Of course, there are subtleties and difficult cases that will make the exact formulation of determinism a tricky matter. But the modality at the core of the notion remains constant. See D. Lewis, "New Work for a Theory of Universals", *Australasian Journal of Philosophy* **61** (1983), 343–77, and J. Earman, *A Primer on Determinism* (Dordrecht: D. Reidel, 1986) for some of the subtleties.

8. One might object that, in the handling of counterfactuals, one has introduced the notion of *closeness*, which seems to be a new primitive. However, closeness is usually understood as a kind of *similarity*, and this notion, it is argued, is one we need *whatever* our views about modality (see, for instance, D. M. Armstrong, *Nominalism and Realism* (Cambridge: Cambridge University Press, 1978) and Lewis, "New Work for a Theory of Universals". In this sense, *similarity* will not be a new primitive.

Chapter 2: Modal language and modal logic

1. For a full discussion and defence of second-order logic for precisely such purposes, see S. Shapiro, *Foundations without Foundationalism* (Oxford: Clarendon Press, 1991).

2. This position is discussed in Chapter 4. It has been defended by A. N. Prior and K. Fine, *Worlds, Times and Selves* (London: Duckworth, 1977) and by G. Forbes, *Languages of Possibility* (Oxford: Blackwell, 1989).

3. There is still some controversy over whether the semantics for second-order theories is really legitimate. See Shapiro, *Foundations without Foundationalism* for a defence of second-order semantics.

4. In fact, logically speaking, only *one* symbol needs to be added. Given negation, $\square$ and $\lozenge$ turn out to be interdefinable, much as $\exists$ and $\forall$ are.

5. Since quantified modal language contains the same terms as the first-order predicate calculus, the terms of the two languages are precisely the same.

6. Note that, since our quantified modal language contains a new predicate E, it contains atomic formulas that are not in the first-order predicate calculus.

7. Certainly, nobody disputes the one modal principle that the argument uses: $\square P$, $\square(P \rightarrow Q)$, therefore $\square Q$. For if P is true no matter how things are, and (If P then Q) is true no matter how things are, then Q is true no matter how things are.

8. Arguments of this form will be examined in more detail in Chapter 3.

9. These difficult issues will be revisited in Chapter 3. Worries such as these form the basis of many of Quine's attacks upon our very grasp of the modality.

10. The argument is whether the effect of such a cardinality quantifier can be had if we allow ourselves first-order logic plus set theory. If set theory is our background theory, then "There are finitely many Fs" can be written in a first-order language as "There is a one-to-one function from the set of Fs to an initial segment of ω." However, since there are non-standard models for first-order set theory on which there are initial segments of ω that contain infinitely many elements, some philosophers claim that, if our background set theory is merely first order, we are still unable to capture the effect of the cardinality quantifier.

11. These sentences and attempts to extend QML to formalize them, will be examined in more detail in Chapter 4.

12. The claim that "There are finitely many Fs" can be expressed even in a first-order theory that quantifies over sets is a contentious one. Second-order theorists point out that there are non-standard models of first-order arithmetic that contain "numbers" n greater than every finite integer. In such models, it can be true that there is a one-to-one correspondence from the set of Fs onto the numbers less than n, but that there are still infinitely many Fs. First-order theorists counter that the existence of such models is irrelevant; in their translation n

refers to an object in *the* set of natural numbers, and not to some thing in whatever set may *play the role* of the set of natural numbers in some non-standard model. The situation is complex and contentious. However, I don't need to take sides in this debate. I simply wish to use this example for purposes of illustration.

13. Note that the following framework is not unique – it is merely there as an illustration of one way in which the possible worlds theorist can express modal truths in a first-order quantified logic.

14. Although the *language* of PWL treats one-place *predicates* of English as having an extra place, this does not immediately imply that it makes the *metaphysical* mistake of making monadic *properties* relational. Whether or not possible worlds turn out to have such metaphysical implications depends upon the metaphysics of possible worlds themselves.

15. Of course, the necessity of identity is a contentious matter. Just because we have written it into the logic of PWL doesn't mean that it cannot or should not be questioned.

16. $\forall x \exists y (Wy \ \& \ Exy)$ says that any object exists at some world. Eaw^* says that a exists at the actual world or, informally, that a actually exists. Finally, $\exists x (Wx \ \& \ Fax) \ \& \ \exists y (Wy \ \& \ \neg Fay)$ says that there is a world at which a is F, and there is a world at which a is not F. Informally, it says that F-ness is a contingent property of a.

17. Some may object that it is excessively naive to take such talk at face value. Others respond that this is overly sceptical – why *shouldn't* we take what we say at face value, at least in the absence of any reason not to?

18. We might have some reservations about this translation. What is this *four*-place predicate "x at w is the same colour as y at v"? How is it related to the familiar two-place predicate "x is the same colour as y"? In Chapter 5, we shall see that the extreme realist about possible worlds has an elegant response to this problem.

19. Even here there is some controversy. Rival systems, such as intuitionistic logic and relevant logic, have their followers.

20. See the earlier discussion of iterated modal operators.

21. Remember, as far as Figure 2.1 is concerned the quantifiers don't range over *everything*; they range only over the things that exist in the big box. After all, the diagram is a representation of a possible situation, and in this possible situation a, b and c are the only things there are.

22. Insisting that models associate with each name in the language an element of D amounts to the assumption that every name of the language has a referent. Of course, this is not a plausible thing to assume about natural language, which contains empty names.

23. D^2 is the set of all ordered pairs whose first and second members are in D. D^3 is the set of all ordered triples whose first, second and third members are in D. D^n in the set of all ordered n-tuples whose first, second, third, …, and nth members are in D. The function is typically called "val".

24. Recall that ordered n-tuples are needed to deal with formulas with many free variables. John and Joe may both satisfy the predicate "x is human", but it is the ordered pair <Joe, John> that satisfies the predicate "x is taller than y". Note that order is needed here: the ordered pair <John, Joe> does not satisfy the predicate because John is not taller than Joe.

25. This is not the only way to write the satisfaction clauses. Another way is to take all formulas to be evaluated relative to infinitely long sequences. Such sequences contain much redundant information and are rather counter-intuitive to work with: the only places in the sequence that are relevant are those that correspond to the nth free variable, and the inductive clauses for the quantifiers are rather counter-intuitive. The restriction that formulas with n free variables are satisfied by n-tuples is a little easier to understand, but the advantage is paid for by an increase in complexity when we come to write down the inductive clauses for the truth-functional connectives. For instance, in a model, the formula $R(x, y)$ & $F(y, z)$ should be satisfied by $<a, b, c>$ iff $R(x, y)$ is satisfied by $<a, b>$ and $F(y, z)$ is satisfied by $<b, c>$. Although the intuitive idea is relatively simple, writing out such inductive clauses for *arbitrary* conjunctions, where the sequences might divide in all kinds of ways, is very hard! Fortunately, since the inductive clauses for conjunctions are not our main focus, we will ignore these technicalities here.

26. See G. Kreisel, "Informal Rigor and Consistency Proofs", in *Problems in the Philosophy of Mathematics* (Amsterdam: North-Holland, 1967). Kreisel's informal proof of this fact uses the fact that first-order logic is complete. Accordingly, his argument cannot be extended to the second-order case. Yet the model-theoretic definition of validity is no less popular here. This suggests that there may be other reasons for accepting the model-theoretic definition, reasons that do not rely on technical matters such as completeness.

27. Obviously, the model we have drawn is a small one, containing as it does only three possible worlds.

28. As before, $M \vDash \varphi$ can be pronounced "φ is true in M".

29. This can be pronounced "φ is true in $<W, ?>$ at w".

30. There is nothing of any significance between these two proposals. Really, they are little more than notational variants of each other.

31. Of course, there's nothing deep going on here. Conceptually, truth in a world in the diagram and truth in the coloured diagram amount to the same thing. No philosophical work is done by this trick, but model theory proceeds a little more smoothly if we adopt it.

32. The phrase "w obeys the same laws as w'" requires clarification. We take it to mean *not* "what is a law at w is a *law* at w'", but "what is a law at w is *true* at w'".

33. A universal relation on a set is one that relates everything in the set to everything else in the set.

34. We note that, in saying when it is that an n-tuple $<a_1, \ldots, a_n>$ satisfies a formula in model $<W, w^*, R, D, d, \text{val}, w>$, there is no restriction upon the objects that appear in $<a_1, \ldots, a_n>$ other than that they all be selected from D. In particular, we have not insisted that they appear in $d(w)$, the domain of w. This means that the semantics allows objects to satisfy formulas in a model at a world, *even if that object does not appear in that world*. This is like saying that, at other possible worlds, Socrates can satisfy or fail to satisfy certain predicates at these worlds, even if Socrates does not exist at these worlds. This may seem surprising; we may feel that, if an object doesn't exist at a world w, it can't satisfy a predicate there. Perhaps "a satisfies $\varphi(x)$" should not even be defined at worlds where a fails to exist? But if we want it to be true that Socrates might not have existed, then there had better be other worlds where Socrates satisfies the predicate $\neg Ex$; but, obviously, he cannot satisfy this predicate at w if he *does* exist at w.

35. These considerations apply to the notion of metaphysical necessity. When thinking about physical necessity, for example, we might come to quite different conclusions about the nature of the accessibility relation.

36. There is a lot more to be said about why we should think that the model theory for the predicate calculus should guide us to the semantic and logical properties of this language. See, for instance, Etchemendy, *The Concept of Logical Consequence*.

37. For one impressive (but difficult) attempt, see C. Chihara, *The Worlds of Possibility* (Oxford: Oxford University Press, 1998).

Chapter 3: Quinian scepticism

1. W. V. Quine, *Word and Object* (Cambridge, MA: MIT Press, 1960).

2. The extension of an n-place predicate is the set of n-tuples that satisfy it. Thus, the extension of "x is taller than y" is the set of all pairs $<a, b>$ with a taller than b.

3. G. Frege, "On Sense and Reference", in *Translations from the Philosophical Writings of Gottlob Frege*, P. Geach & M. Black (eds) (Oxford: Blackwell, 1980).

4. The scare quotes are there to remind the reader that, for all that has been said so far, an "intensional object" is simply an object that is not extensional, that is, not an individual, set or truth-value.

5. For instance, Carnap's individual concepts: R. Carnap, *Meaning and Necessity* (Chicago, IL: University of Chicagor Press, 1947).

6. This is not just a feature of the system that we decided to focus on. The formal systems that were developed in the 1940s and 1950s lacked definite description. Indeed, many of these systems lacked proper names. The *only* terms of these languages were the variables.

7. In fact, because of the logical properties of "taller", this Russellian clause is actually redundant here.

8. N. Wilson, *The Concept of Language* (Toronto: University of Toronto Press, 1959).

9. This, for instance, was Hintikka's attitude: see J. Hintikka, "The Modes of Modality", *Acta Philosophica Fennica* 16 (1963), 65–81, reprinted in M. Loux (ed.), *The Possible and the Actual* (Ithaca, NY: Cornell University Press, 1979).

10. W. V. Quine, "Reference and Modality", in *From a Logical Point of View*, 139–59 (New York: Harper and Row, 1961), reprinted in L. Linsky (ed.), *Reference and Modality* (Oxford: Oxford University Press, 1971).

11. The strength and plausibility of this principle depends heavily upon the range of properties we take ourselves to be quantifying over in this principle. Are the properties just *qualitative* ones – properties such as *being red*, *having mass* and the like? If so, the principle is contentious. Or are non-qualitative properties included, such as "being a member of set S", and "being the brother of a"? Indeed, are properties such as "being identical to b" included? In that case the principle is true, but trivial.

12. This principle is plausible *whatever* we take the range of properties to be.

13. L. Linsky, "Reference, Essentialism and Modalism", in Linsky (ed.), *Reference and Modality*, 89.

14. That is, sentences that contain no free variables.

15. This solution is essentially Smullyan's in A. F. Smullyan, "Modality and Description", *Journal of Symbolic Logic* **13**(1) (1948), 31–7.
16. Linsky, *Reference and Modality*, 11.

Chapter 4: Modalism

1. Recall that w^* is the possible worlds theorist's name for the actual world.
2. Scare quotes are there because, for the modalist, this cannot literally be the right way to understand our problem: there are no possible objects.
3. That is, modal operators that appear within the scope of other modal operators.
4. Again, for simplicity, we are ignoring the complications of the accessibility relation here.
5. Peacocke first introduced these operators in C. Peacocke, "Necessity and Truth Theories", *Journal of Philosophical Logic* 7 (1978), 473–500. They are essentially the modal analogues of the temporal Vlach operators introduced by F. Vlach, "'Now' and 'Then': A Formal Study in the Logic of Tense Anaphora", UCLA Dissertation, University Microfilms, Ann Arbor, Michigan. See also K. Fine, "Postscript: Prior on the Construction of Possible Worlds and Instants", in Prior and Fine, *Worlds, Times and Selves*, 116–61, and Forbes, *Languages of Possibility*.
6. It's empty because nothing has yet been stored in the sequence.
7. Strictly, this is for some world v such that w^*Rv. But for simplicity, let us suppose that we are working with models where the accessibility relation is universal, so we can ignore this complication. Do not forget that we gained the insight that the accessibility relation should be universal by appealing to intuitions about possible worlds, so there are real questions as to whether the modalist can help himself to this simplification.
8. Remember, quantifiers are restricted to the objects that exist at the world of evaluation.
9. See Forbes, *Languages of Possibility*, 91.
10. Peacocke, "Necessity and Truth Theories".

Chapter 5: Extreme realism

1. We should note that the overall theoretical utility of a theory of possible worlds may go beyond the topic of modality. Lewis, for instance, uses his possible worlds to analyse the notions of a proposition and a property – two concepts that are quite removed from modality. Here, we are concerned only with notions and concepts from modality, but there is more to be said in favour of extreme realism than we say here.
2. Qualitative properties are those such as *being square*, *having a mass of 3 kg*, and *being happy*. Non-qualitative properties are properties such as *being identical to a* and *having F essentially*.
3. See, for instance, W. Lycan, "The Trouble with Possible Worlds", in Loux, *The Possible and the Actual*.
4. This is analogous to questions about what it is for one and the same object to exist at different *times*.
5. S. Kripke, *Naming and Necessity* (Oxford: Blackwell, 1980).
6. See A. Hazen, "Counterpart Theoretic Semantics for Modal Languages", *Journal of Philosophy* 76 (1979), 319–38.

7. A. Plantinga, *The Nature of Necessity* (Oxford: Clarendon Press, 1974).
8. Lewis's language will not quite be the possible worlds language PWL that we met in Chapter 2. PWL talked of one and the same object existing at different worlds, while Lewis prefers to talk of counterparts. See D. Lewis, "Counterpart Theory and Quantified Modal Logic", *Journal of Philosophy* 65 (1968), 113–26 for the details.
9. Sets of worlds rather than worlds because the quantification is naturally understood as ranging over possibilities rather than whole possible worlds. Whereas a possibility is a complete way the world could have been, possibilities are thought of as being incomplete. Incomplete possibilities are typically treated as *sets* of worlds: the possibility that *P* is the set of worlds at which *P* is true.
10. Note that although I have expressed these statements in English, they can all be easily formalized in a quantified predicate language.
11. Recall that w^* is our name for the actual world.
12. Later in this chapter we shall question whether this really does hold of extreme realism.
13. D. Lewis, *Counterfactuals* (Oxford: Blackwell, 1973).
14. One should note that this is a stronger claim. "Every single object might not have existed" does not entail "There might have been nothing." Proof: consider a possible worlds model where no one object exists at every single world, yet every world contains something.
15. C. D. Broad, *Examination of McTaggart's Philosophy*, vol 1 (Cambridge: Cambridge University Press, 1933). More recently, D. M. Armstrong, *A Combinatorial Theory of Possibility* (Cambridge: Cambridge University Press, 1989), 16, and W. H. Newton-Smith, *The Structure of Time* (London: Routledge & Kegan Paul, 1980), Ch. 4 accept such possibilities.
16. Lewis, *Counterfactuals*, 87.
17. This section was written with John Divers. My thanks to him for permitting me to use this material here.
18. D. Lewis, *On the Plurality of Worlds* (Oxford: Blackwell, 1986), 86.
19. *Ibid.*, 88.
20. *Ibid.*, 88–9.

Chapter 6: Quiet moderate realism

1. Various versions of linguistic realism will be examined in Chapter 7.
2. B. Skyrms, "Tractarian Nominalism", *Philosophical Studies* 40 (1981), 199–206.
3. R. M. Adams, "Theories of Actuality", *Noûs* 8 (1974), 211–31.
4. Plantinga, *The Nature of Necessity*.
5. R. Stalnaker, "Possible Worlds", *Noûs* 10 (1976), 65–75.
6. Note that this is different from saying that the worlds themselves must be complete.
7. "More or less" rather than "exactly" because "*a* is *F*" is true at a world *w* when *w* contains a counterpart of *a* that is *F*, rather than *w* containing *a* and *a*'s being *F* there.
8. Note that although such considerations are reasons to believe in the *existence* of propositions, they shed very little light on the *nature* of propositions. A brief survey of the literature reveals that there are many different theories of proposition.

Indeed, there is one theory on which propositions themselves are nothing more than sets of worlds. Clearly, such a theory is out of the question in this context, where we are looking to construct worlds out of propositions.

9. Although they are typically thought of as being complete, in Chapter 7 we will question whether it is really necessary for the theorist's purposes to always take them to be complete.

10. Indeed, if the arguments of Chapter 5 were correct, and *possibility* must be taken as a primitive by the extreme realist, then the number is only one.

11. See, for example, Plantinga, *The Nature of Necessity* and "Actualism and Possible Worlds", *Theoria* **42** (1976), 139–60.

12. Plantinga, "Actualism and Possible Worlds".

13. Such an attractive view of states of affairs has been defended and developed by Armstrong; see, for example, D. M. Armstrong, *A World of States of Affairs* (Cambridge: Cambridge University Press, 1997).

14. The view that there are worlds that differ only over which objects have which properties is called *haecceitism*. Haecceitism will be studied in more detail in Chapter 7. Note that not all combinatorialists accept haecceitism (Armstrong, for example, rejects it) even though it seems to follow naturally from the basic combinatorialist insight.

15. However, see Armstrong, *A Combinatorial Theory of Possibility*, for an interesting attempt to restrict the principle of recombination by allowing only those recombinations of elements which do not overlap to count as a possible world.

16. See, for instance, *ibid*.

17. Lewis, *On the Plurality of Worlds*, 174–91.

18. Beware. There is quite a different definition of "internal" in the philosophical literature. For some philosophers, an internal relation is one where the mere existence of the relata entails that the relation holds between them. Note, moreover, that the intrinsic properties relevant here are the *qualitative* intrinsic properties, properties such as *is blue* and *is square* rather than properties such as *is identical to b*.

19. Note that this definition of "external" is not Lewis's. For Lewis, a relation is external if it does not supervene on the natures of the relata, but *does* supervene on the nature of the sum. I do not think the distinction plays a role in his argument, however, so I adopt the simpler, two-fold, classification.

20. Given that Lewis's internal/external distinction is not exhaustive, it is not entirely clear that he is justified in concentrating only on these two branches.

21. Lewis, *On the Plurality of Worlds*, 177.

22. *Ibid.*, 177.

23. *Ibid.*, 178.

24. See P. van Inwagen, "Two Concepts of Possible Worlds", *Midwest Studies in Philosophy* **11** (1986), 185–213.

25. Lewis, *On the Plurality of Worlds*, 179.

26. See van Inwagen, "Two Concepts of Possible Worlds".

27. Lewis, *On the Plurality of Worlds*, 27–69.

28. *Ibid.*, 180.

29. See Chapter 5.

30. Lewis, *On the Plurality of Worlds*, 180.

Chapter 7: Possible worlds as sets of sentences

1. Lewis, *On the Plurality of Worlds*, 165–74.
2. Carnap, *Meaning and Necessity*.
3. R. Jeffrey, *The Logic of Decision* (New York: McGraw Hill, 1965).
4. J. Hintikka, *Models for Modality: Selected Essays* (Dordrecht: Reidel, 1969).
5. The world-making language is *so* divorced from actual languages that one might wonder whether the theory really ought to be called linguistic at all. But this is the name that philosophers have labelled such theories and I have been unable to think of a better one.
6. Note that adopting this convention limits the linguistic theorist's analytic ambitions. Since *properties* form part of the fundamental constituents of his possible worlds, the linguistic theorist is unable to analyse the notion of a property in possible worlds terms. This difficulty may not be insurmountable, however. Perhaps, when physics is completed, we will have predicates $P_1, P_2, \ldots, P_n$ for all the fundamental kinds of things there are. Any actually instantiated complex property could be analysed in terms of these predicates. So it may well be that, on the successful completion of physics, the linguistic theorist will be able to adopt a language containing only the predicates $P_1, P_2, \ldots, P_n$, which has all the expressive power of the Lagadonian language above, but that does not require him to postulate such things as properties.
7. Lewis suggests this proposal on the linguistic theorist's behalf.
8. Alien properties, properties that cannot be analysed in terms of actually instantiated properties, were explained and discussed in Chapter 5.
9. See Chapter 5.
10. See Lewis, *On the Plurality of Worlds*; Armstrong, *A Combinatorial Theory of Possibility*, 58–9; D. Kaplan, "How to Russell a Frege-Church", *Journal of Philosophy* 72 (1975), 716–29; and Skyrms, "Tractarian Nominalism".
11. Lewis, *On the Plurality of Worlds*, 162.
12. Although Shoemaker accepts it.
13. Lewis, *On the Plurality of Worlds*, 162–5; and P. Bricker, "Reducing Possible Worlds to Language", *Philosophical Studies* 52 (1987), 331–55.
14. As Skyrms has done in "Tractarian Nominalism".
15. Lewis, *On the Plurality of Worlds*, 163–4.
16. R. Stalnaker, *Inquiry* (Cambridge, MA: MIT Press, 1984), 119.
17. J. Hintikka, "Situations, Possible Worlds, and Attitudes", *Synthese* 54 (1983), 153–62.

Further reading

Collections
Two anthologies of important papers are:
1. L. Linsky (ed.), *Reference and Modality*, (Oxford: Oxford University Press, 1971). This book contains many important papers written in the early development of modal logic and possible worlds semantics when philosophers such as Quine were questioning the very coherence of modal notions.
2. M. Loux, *The Possible and The Actual* (Ithaca, NY: Cornell University Press, 1979). By the time of the papers collected here, the lessons from possible worlds semantics have been learned, but questions are being asked about the metaphysical picture which now emerges. This anthology contains early versions of many of the key theories of possible worlds.

Books
Three useful books on modality and possible worlds are:
1. A. Plantinga, *The Nature of Necessity* (Oxford: Clarendon Press, 1974). This book contains both a nice, accessible introduction to modality and an interesting and advanced theory of possible worlds.
2. D. Lewis, *On the Plurality of Worlds* (Oxford: Blackwell, 1986). Although essentially a defence of Lewis's version of realism, there is much here that is important to all. Chapter 1 contains an exposition of the various analytic benefits that a possible worlds ontology can bring, benefits that go beyond the modal applications discussed in this book. Throughout the book, Lewis deals with advanced issues in a clear and accessible way.
3. J. Divers, *Possible Worlds* (London: Routledge, 2002). This contains a recent, deep and comprehensive treatment of the possible worlds debate.

Chapter 1: Introduction to modality
Useful philosophical and conceptual work done by modal concepts and possible worlds is discussed in a number of areas. D. Lewis, "Causation", *Journal of Philosophy* 70 (1973), 556–67, shows how counterfactuals can be used in the analysis of causation; D. Lewis, *Counterfactuals* (Oxford: Blackwell, 1973) and R. Stalnaker

"A Theory of Conditionals", in *Studies in Logical Theory,* N. Rescher (ed.) (Oxford: Blackwell, 1968), 98–112 discuss the role of possible worlds in the semantics of counterfactuals themselves. For discussions of *supervenience* with particular applications to the philosophy of mind, see the range of essays in J. Kim, *Supervenience and Mind* (Cambridge: Cambridge University Press, 1993). For an account of the possible worlds approach towards supervenience, see D. Lewis, *On the Plurality of Worlds,* 14–17. J. Divers "Supervenience for Operators", *Synthese* **106** (1996), 103–112, contains an interesting attempt to formulate such supervenience claims without appealing to possible worlds.

Although our interest in this book has been with the applications of possible worlds to modality, much early interest in possible worlds arose with their semantic applications. See, R. Carnap, *Meaning and Necessity* (Chicago, IL: University of Chicago Press, 1947), R. Montague "Pragmatics and Intensional Logics", *Synthese* **22** (1970), 68–94 and D. Lewis "General Semantics", *Synthese* **22** (1970), 18–67. Possible worlds also have ontological applications: it has been proposed that propositions be identified with possible worlds and that properties be identified with sets of possible objects – see D. Lewis, *On the Plurality of Worlds,* 20–69 for a thorough discussion of such identifications.

The realism–anti-realism debate rears its head in most areas of philosophy, and modality is no exception. Although much of our modal thought and talk has the appearance and feel of thought and talk about something objective, there are nevertheless many who find projectivist, conventionalist and fictionalist views of modality attractive. For a recent *projectivist* view about such thought and talk, see S. Blackburn, "Morals and Modals", in *Fact, Science and Morality: Essays on A. J. Ayer's Language, Truth and Logic,* G. MacDonald and C. Wright (eds), 119–42 (Oxford: Blackwell, 1986). *Conventionalism* about the modal has recently been resurrected by A. Sidelle, *Necessity, Essence and Individuation: a Defense of Conventionalism* (Ithaca, NY: Cornell University Press, 1993). Recently, *fictionalism* seems to have become the most popular anti-realist approach to the modal. For a selection of papers, see G. Rosen "Modal Fictionalism", *Mind* **99** (1990), 327–54; G. Rosen "Modal Fictionalism Fixed", *Analysis* **55** (1995), 67–73; and J. Divers, "A Modal Fictionalist Result", *Noûs* **33** (1999), 317–46.

Chapter 2: Modal language and modal logic

Possible worlds semantics seems to have been invented by a number of philosophers at roughly the same time. Two papers that are easy to get hold of are S. Kripke, "Semantical Considerations of Modal Logic", *Acta Philosophica Fennica* **16** (1963), 83–94, reprinted in Linsky, *Reference and Modality,* 63–72; and J. Hintikka, "The Modes of Modality", *Acta Philosophica Fennica* **16** (1963), 65–82, reprinted in Loux, *The Possible and The Actual,* 65–89. R. Girle, *Possible Worlds* (Chesham: Acumen, 2003) is a very readable and helpful introduction to the use of possible worlds in both modal and non-modal logics. For those comfortable with first-order modal logic, G. E. Hughes and M. J. Cresswell, *A New Introduction to Modal Logic* (London: Routledge, 1996) and M. Fitting and R. L. Mendelson *First-order Modal Logic* (Dordrecht: Kluwer, 1998) are two accessible books that guide the reader further into the deeper technicalities of modal logic. A deep and ingenious attempt to justify the use of possible worlds semantics while rejecting the existence of such things as possible worlds is C. Chihara, *The Worlds of Possibility* (Oxford: Oxford University Press, 1998).

Chapter 3: Quinian scepticism

The papers in Linsky, *Reference and Modality*, contain philosophers' early responses to Quinian scepticism about the modal. For good material on compositional semantics, see D. Lewis, "Compositional Semantics". See also D. Lewis, "Tensions", in *Semantics and Philosophy*, M. K. Munitz and P. K. Unger (eds) (New York: New York University Press, 1974), reprinted in Lewis, *Philosophical Papers*, vol. 1 (Oxford: Oxford University Press, 1983), 250–60. Chapter 10 of S. Haack, *Philosophy of Logics* (Cambridge: Cambridge University Press, 1978) contains a good summary of the debate about Quine's worries about modality. For more recent work on a Quinian approach to modality, see J. P. Burgess, "Quinus ab Omni Naevo Vindicatus", in *Meaning and Reference*, Ali A. Kazmi (ed.), *Canadian Journal of Philosophy Supplementary Volume* 23 (1997), 25–65; S. Neale "On a Milestone of Empiricism", in *Knowledge, Language and Logic: Questions for Quine*, A. Orenstein and P. Kotatko (eds) (Dordrecht: Kluwer, 2000), 237–346; B. van Fraassen, "The Only Necessity is Verbal Necessity", *Journal of Philosophy* 74 (1977), 71–85; and P. Boghossian, "Analyticity Reconsidered", *Noûs* 30 (1996), 360–91.

Chapter 4: Modalism

For an early exposition of the modalist's position, see K. Fine, "Postscript", in *Worlds, Times and Selves*, A. N. Prior and K. Fine (London: Duckworth, 1977). Modalism has been most comprehensively developed and defended by G. Forbes in his books *The Metaphysics of Modality* (Oxford: Clarendon Press, 1985) and, particularly, *The Languages of Possibility* (Oxford: Blackwell, 1989). See also J. Melia "Against Modalism", *Philosophical Studies* 68 (1992), 49–66 and "Melia on Modalism", *Philosophical Studies* 68 (1992), 57–63.

Chapter 5: Extreme realism

Extreme realism is defended with great vigour in Lewis, *On the Plurality of Worlds*. Lewis's original proposal for translating modal claims into his theory of counterparts appears in his "Counterpart Theory and Quantified Modal Logic", *Journal of Philosophy* 65 (1968), 113–26. See also his "Postscripts to 'Counterpart Theory and Quantified Modal Logic'", in *Philosophical Papers: Volume 1*, 39–46 (Oxford: Oxford University Press, 1983) and A. Hazen "Counterpart Theoretic Semantics for Modal Logic", *Journal of Philosophy* 76 (1979), 319–38 for further details and developments. Certain statements about entities that appear across worlds or outside worlds, such as propositions or numbers, cannot sensibly be translated using Lewis's original translation scheme, but J. Divers, "A Genuine Realist Theory of Advanced Modalizing", *Mind* 108 (1999), 217–39 gives Lewis a way out. For further details on the worry that Lewis's view about possible worlds forces him to omit genuine possibilities, see J. Bigelow and R. Pargetter, "Beyond the Blank Stare", *Theoria* 53 (1987), 97–114 and J. Divers, *Possible Worlds*, 93–100.

One argument not examined in the text claims that the principle of recombination leads to a kind of paradox. See P. Forrest and D. Armstrong, "An Argument against David Lewis's Theory of Possible Worlds", *Australasian Journal of Philosophy* 62 (1984), 164–8; D. Nolan "Recombination Unbound", *Philosophical Studies* 84 (1996), 239–62; and J. Divers, *Possible Worlds*, 100–3.

The charge that Lewis's extreme modal realism smuggles in a hidden notion of possibility has been made by many; see S. Shalkowski, "The Ontological Ground of

Alethic Modality", *Philosophical Review* 103 (1994), 669–88; W. Lycan "Review of D. Lewis, 'On the Plurality of Worlds'" *Journal of Philosophy* 85 (1988), 42–7; and J. Divers and J. Melia, "The Analytic Limit of Genuine Modal Realism", *Mind* 111 (2002), 15–36.

Chapter 6: Quiet moderate realism

Many versions of quiet moderate realism can be found in M. Loux (ed.), *The Possible and the Actual*. In this collection, R. M. Adams, "Theories of Actuality", identifies worlds with sets of propositions, R. Stalnaker, "Possible Worlds", identifies worlds with abstract properties, and A. Plantinga, "Actualism and Possible Worlds", identifies worlds with states of affairs. An interesting development of the view that worlds are abstract properties is P. Forrest, "Ways Worlds Could Be", *Australasian Journal of Philosophy* 64 (1986), 15–24. A developed and detailed account of combinatorialist principles can be found in D. M. Armstrong, *A Combinatorial Theory of Possibility* (Cambridge: Cambridge University Press, 1989), although in this book Armstrong appears to adopt a *fictionalist* attitude towards worlds; see D. Lewis, "Review of D. A. Armstrong, 'A Combinatorial Theory of Possibility'", *Australasian Journal of Philosophy* 74 (1992), 211–24.

It has been argued that the ontology postulated by quiet moderate realism is subject to a Cantorian-style paradox. See P. Grim, "There is no Set of all Truths", *Analysis* 44 (1984), 206–8; S. Bringsjord, "Are there Set Theoretic Possible Worlds?", *Analysis* 45 (1985), 64; and J. Divers, *Possible Worlds*, 243–56.

For further reading on Lewis's argument against quiet moderate realism, see P. van Inwagen's excellent "Two Concepts of Possible Worlds", in *Midwest Studies in Philosophy, Vol. 11, Studies in Essentialism*, P. French, T. Uehling and H. Wettstein (eds), 185–213 (Minneapolis, MN: Minnesota University Press, 1986), which is a superb dissection of and counter to Lewis's argument against quiet moderate realisms; and M. Jubien, "Could this be Magic?", *Philosophical Review* 100 (1991), 249–67.

Chapter 7: Possible worlds as sets of sentences

B. Skyrms, "Tractarian Nominalism", *Philosophical Studies* 40 (1981), 199–206 develops a combinatorial scheme that Lewis has given a linguistic gloss. A number of problems for such a theory can be found in P. Bricker, "Reducing Possible Worlds to Language", *Philosophical Studies* 52 (1987), 331–55 and D. Lewis, *The Plurality of Worlds*, 142–63. T. Roy, "In Defence of Linguistic Ersatzism", *Philosophical Studies* 80 (1995), 217–42 and J. Melia, "Reducing Possibilities to Language", *Analysis* 61 (2001), 19–29, try to show a way out for the linguistic theory. However, T. Sider "The Ersatz Pluriverse", *Journal of Philosophy* 99 (2002), 279–315 contains a novel and promising suggestion for developing the linguistic theorist's ideas.

Index